2012

Preliminary Overview of the Economies
of Latin America and the Caribbean

UNITED NATIONS

ECLAC

Alicia Bárcena
Executive Secretary

Antonio Prado
Deputy Executive Secretary

Juan Alberto Fuentes
Chief Economic Development Division

Ricardo Pérez
Chief Documents and Publications Division

The *Preliminary Overview of the Economies of Latin America and the Caribbean* is an annual publication prepared by the Economic Development Division of the Economic Commission for Latin America and the Caribbean (ECLAC). This 2012 edition was prepared under the supervision of Juan Alberto Fuentes, Chief of the Division.

In the preparation of this edition, the Economic Development Division was assisted by the Statistics Division, the ECLAC subregional headquarters in Mexico City and Port of Spain, and the Commission's country offices in Bogota, Brasilia, Buenos Aires, Montevideo and Washington, D.C.

The regional analyses were prepared by Juan Alberto Fuentes with input from the following experts: Luis Felipe Jiménez, Cameron Daneshvar y Seung-jin Baek (external sector), Ricardo Martner and Andrea Podestá (fiscal policy), Ramón Pineda, Rodrigo Cárcamo, Benjamin Rae and Alejandra Acevedo (monetary, exchange-rate and macroprudential policies), Sandra Manuelito (activity and prices) and Jürgen Weller (employment and wages). The economic projections were produced by Sandra Manuelito and Claudio Aravena. Vianka Aliaga, Leandro Cabello, Jazmín Chiu, Ivonne González, Michael Hanni and Carolina Serpell were responsible for the processing and presentation of the statistical data and graphical presentations.

The country notes are based on studies conducted by the following experts: Olga Lucía Acosta, Nohora Forero and Juan Carlos Ramírez (Colombia), Dillon Alleyne (Jamaica and Suriname), Rodrigo Cárcamo (Bolivarian Republic of Venezuela), Cameron Daneshvar (Paraguay), Maria Kristina Eisele (Honduras), Randolph Gilbert (Haiti), Michael Hendrickson (Bahamas and Belize), Juan Pablo Jiménez (Uruguay), Luis Felipe Jiménez (Chile), Cornelia Kaldewei (Ecuador), Sandra Manuelito (Peru), Rodolfo Minzer (Costa Rica and Panamá), Carlos Mussi (Brazil), Ramón Padilla (Mexico), Machel Pantin (Trinidad and Tobago), Willard Phillips (Barbados and Eastern Caribbean Monetary Union), Benjamin Rae (Plurinational State of Bolivia), Juan Carlos Rivas (Guatemala), Indira Romero (Cuba), Daniel Vega (Argentina), Francisco Villareal (El Salvador), Kohei Yoshida (Guyana) and Willy Zapata (Nicaragua and the Dominican Republic).

The country notes are available on line at www.eclac.org.
The cut-off date for the information presented in this publication was 30 November 2012.

Note:
The following symbols have been used in the tables shown in the Survey:
Three dots (…) indicate that data are not available or are not separately reported.
A dash (-) indicates that the amount is nil or negligible.
A full stop (.) is used to indicate decimals.
The word "dollars" refers to United States dollars unless otherwise specified.

United Nations Publication
ISBN: 978-92-1-121826-8 • ISSN printed version: 1014-7810
E-ISBN: 978-92-1-055959-1
LC/G.2555-P • Sales No.: E.13.II.G.2
Copyright © United Nations, January 2013. All rights reserved
Printed in Santiago, Chile • 2012-1015

Contents

Tables

Figures

Executive summary

The global economic crisis has had a negative, albeit not dramatic, impact in the region

The global economy slowed significantly in 2012, amid recession in Europe caused by financial, fiscal and competitiveness imbalances, especially in the eurozone, as well as the slowdown in China and moderate growth in the United States. Growth rates for output and global trade fell and capital flows to developing countries shrank and became more volatile.

The downturn was transmitted to Latin America and the Caribbean mainly through the trade channel. With the European Union in recession and China's economy slowing in 2012, the region's exports to the European Union shrank by 4.9% in value terms and those to China, by 1.7%. By contrast, exports to the United States increased by 4.8% thanks to modest growth in that economy, and intraregional exports climbed 1.4%.[1] Growth in export values tailed off sharply for Latin America and the Caribbean overall, from 23.9% in 2011 to an estimated 1.6% in 2012.[2]

The impact was differentiated within the region. Hydrocarbon-exporting countries, together with Mexico and the Central American and Caribbean countries, much of whose goods and services exports go to the United States, felt a smaller impact since many of them increased their exports to that economy and, in some cases, to Europe and China as well. Other South American countries, which ship a larger share of their exports —especially of natural resources— to China and the European Union, suffered a heavier impact, with

exports to both destinations falling sharply for some of them. Inbound tourism in the region, especially in Central America and the Caribbean, returned a positive growth rate in 2012 and remittances, mainly from the United States, also rose in these countries. Conversely, remittances fell in countries, like Ecuador and Colombia, for which Spain is a larger emigrant destination.

Another impact of the cooling global economy was the downturn in terms of trade for the region overall, although countries that export mainly hydrocarbons and oils and oilseeds were able to avoid this impact, thanks to still high prices in the first case and a climate-driven spike in prices in the second. With terms of trade down or stable in most of the region's countries, the expansion in export value was attributable mainly to higher export volumes and not, as in recent years, to higher prices. Brazil was an exception to this trend, since its export values shrank, reflecting a fall in prices and more or less stable total export volumes.

The foregoing trends translated into a reduction in the goods trade surplus on the regional balance of payments between 2011 and 2012 (from 1.3% to 0.9% of GDP), which in turn shows up in a wider current account deficit (from -1.3% to -1.6% of GDP) for the region overall and especially for most of the South American countries. The deterioration in the current account position was more marked in the case of mineral- and metal-exporters, whose imports were also pushed up by domestic demand.

Conversely, Mexico yielded a narrower current account deficit in 2012, as a result of smaller outflows on the factor income account, and the trade and current account balances of the Central American countries showed little change, although their current account deficit remain high at around 7% of GDP.

---

[1]   These growth rates refer to data for the period January-September 2012.
[2]   This figure corresponds to the variation in export values for countries which have reported data for both years.

Global financial instability led to smaller inflows of short-term capital and a more volatile exchange rate in Brazil and Mexico, but eased pressures towards currency appreciation

Amid global financial instability, short-term net capital inflows into Latin America and the Caribbean were down in 2012 and exchange rates were more volatile in Brazil and Mexico, the region's two largest countries and among the most integrated into the international financial markets. International reserves continued to accumulate in the region overall, but more slowly than in 2011. Pressures towards currency appreciation eased in several countries as the current account position deteriorated and capital inflows decreased —in some cases as a result of regulations or a reduction in sovereign bond issues abroad (although private issues increased). The currencies depreciated in both nominal and real terms in Brazil and Mexico,[3] but in other countries local currencies continued to appreciate despite currency-market interventions and a build-up, in some cases of over 1% of GDP, in international reserves. Only Argentina, the Bolivarian Republic of Venezuela and Chile saw a decline in international reserves of any significance in 2012.

Monetary policy was slightly expansionary

In most of the countries monetary policy was geared towards offsetting the negative impact of shrinking external demand on economic activity. Generally speaking, the countries avoided policies —such as interest rate hikes or other types of measure aimed at controlling monetary aggregates— that could choke credit growth and domestic demand, despite an uptick in inflation caused in part by the rise in food prices starting in September 2012. Inflation did temporarily breach the upper limit of the band in countries which run inflation-targeting schemes, such as Mexico and Peru, but the rate for the region overall in 2012 (5.8%) was lower than in 2011 (6.9%).

Efforts continued to strengthen macroprudential policies through changes to legal reserve requirements, sometimes to promote the use of national currencies (as in Paraguay, Peru, the Plurinational State of Bolivia and Uruguay) or to prevent overborrowing by households (Colombia). Reforms were also made to financial regulations to improve countercyclical provisioning (Ecuador), reduce

interest rate risks (Bahamas, Paraguay and Ecuador) or expand central bank powers (Argentina and, to a lesser degree, Guatemala).

The fiscal position deteriorated in most of the countries, but fiscal policies have remained predominantly prudent

With only a few exceptions, the gap between income and expenditure rose in most of the countries as spending rose faster (1 percentage point of GDP) than income (0.6 percentage points). However, analysis of fiscal balances alongside the economic cycle in the region suggests that in general a prudent fiscal policy stance has been maintained in 2012.

The higher spending helped to maintain the momentum of domestic demand, especially consumption, with current spending rising by 0.6 GDP percentage points and capital spending 0.5 GDP points. In the case of natural-resources-exporters, the drop in non-tax income was offset by a rise in tax income on the strength of buoyant domestic demand but, in countries where revenues increased (13 of 19), the rise was usually quite moderate. Meanwhile, the various tax measures or reforms being pursued in several countries (Chile, the Dominican Republic, Ecuador, El Salvador, Guatemala, Panama and Peru) should increase their tax burden in 2013.

Debt levels rose only slightly and did not pose a threat to fiscal sustainability in the Latin American countries. The fiscal deterioration was larger in the Caribbean, however, where the overall fiscal deficit widened from 3.6% to 4.0% of GDP. The fiscal position worsened not only in the service-exporting economies of the Caribbean, but also in the natural resources-exporting countries.

The region's economy proved resilient, despite the global economic downturn

The economic activity arising from the interaction between global economic deterioration, the region's pattern of specialization and the policy mix implemented by the governments suggested that Latin America and the Caribbean has continued to show some resilience to external shocks. In particular, the region's rate of GDP growth (3.1%) exceeded global growth (2.2%), unemployment eased down from 6.9% in 2011 in 6.4% in 2012, and real wages rose (see figure 1 and table A-21 in the statistical annex). Most of the English- and Dutch-speaking Caribbean countries, which have taken longer to rebound from the global financial crisis of 2008-2009, returned growth rates in 2012 that were still low, but nevertheless positive and slightly up on 2011 (1.1% versus 0.4%).

---

[3]   Comparison of the daily average nominal exchange rate against the dollar for January-November 2012 with the daily average for the year-earlier period shows a depreciation of 7% in the Mexico peso and 17.3% in the Brazilian real.

Figure 1
LATIN AMERICA AND THE CARIBBEAN: ECONOMIC GROWTH, EMPLOYMENT AND UNEMPLOYMENT, 2000-2012
(Percentages)

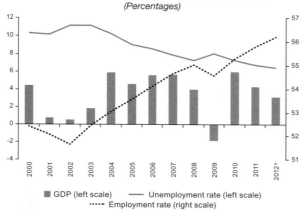

■ GDP (left scale) —— Unemployment rate (left scale)
····· Employment rate (right scale)

Source: Economic Commission for Latin America and the Caribbean (ECLAC), on the basis of official figures.
a Estimates.

Table 1
LATIN AMERICA AND THE CARIBBEAN: VARIATION IN TOTAL GROSS DOMESTIC PRODUCT
(Millions of dollars at constant 2005 prices)

	2010	2011	2012[a]	2013[b]
Argentina	9.2	8.9	2.2	3.9
Bolivia (Plurinational State of)	4.1	5.2	5.0	5.0
Brazil	7.5	2.7	1.2	4.0
Chile	6.1	6.0	5.5	4.8
Colombia	4.0	5.9	4.5	4.5
Costa Rica	4.7	4.2	5.0	3.5
Cuba	2.4	2.7	3.0	3.5
Dominican Republic	7.8	4.5	3.8	3.0
Ecuador	3.6	7.8	4.8	3.5
El Salvador	1.4	1.5	1.2	2.0
Guatemala	2.9	3.9	3.3	3.5
Haiti	-5.4	5.6	2.5	6.0
Honduras	2.8	3.6	3.5	3.5
Mexico	5.6	3.9	3.8	3.5
Nicaragua	3.1	5.1	4.0	4.5
Panama	7.6	10.6	10.5	7.5
Paraguay	13.1	4.4	-1.8	8.5
Peru	8.8	6.9	6.2	6.0
Uruguay	8.9	5.7	3.8	4.0
Venezuela (Bolivarian Republic of)	-1.5	4.2	5.3	2.0
Subtotal Central America (9 countries)	**4.1**	**4.3**	**4.2**	**3.8**
Subtotal South America (10 countries)	**6.5**	**4.5**	**2.7**	**4.1**
Antigua and Barbuda	-7.9	-5.0	0.9	2.4
Bahamas	0.2	1.6	2.5	3.0
Barbados	0.2	0.6	0.2	1.0
Belice	2.9	2.5	4.2	2.3
Dominica	0.9	-0.3	1.6	1.7
Granada	0.0	1.0	0.2	1.2
Guyana	4.4	5.4	3.8	4.9
Jamaica	-1.5	1.3	-0.2	0.1
Saint Kitts and Nevis	-2.4	2.1	-0.8	1.8
Saint Lucia	0.4	1.3	0.9	1.9
Saint Vincent and the Grenadines	-2.8	0.1	1.5	1.5
Suriname	7.3	4.5	3.6	4.7
Trinidad and Tobago	0.0	-1.4	1.0	2.5
Subtotal the Caribbean	**-0.1**	**0.4**	**1.1**	**2.0**
Latin America and the Caribbean	**5.9**	**4.3**	**3.1**	**3.8**

Source: Economic Commission for Latin America and the Caribbean (ECLAC), on the basis of official figures.
a Estimates.
b Projections.

The regional performance was heavily weighted by slower growth in two of the largest economies,[4] Argentina (2.2% in 2012 compared with 8.9% in 2011) and Brazil (1.2% versus 2.7%, respectively). Not including these two countries, the region's GDP rose by 4.3%, which was not far from the rate without those countries in 2011 (4.5%). Mexico's economy expanded 3.8% and several countries posted rates of 5% or more, including the Bolivarian Republic of Venezuela (5.3%), Chile (5.5%), Costa Rica (5%), Peru (6.2%) and the Plurinational State of Bolivia (5%). Panama was again the region's fastest-growing economy (10.5%). The other economies in Latin America and the Caribbean expanded by between 1% and 5%, except for Paraguay, Saint Kitts and Nevis and Jamaica, which registered negative growth. Central America overall achieved growth of 4.2%, South America 2.7% and the Caribbean 1.1% (see table 1).

With external demand weakening, growth in the region was driven by domestic demand, fuelled partly by monetary or fiscal policy measures in most of the countries. The rise in demand was chiefly a reflection of consumption, with public consumption making a larger contribution than in 2011, consistently with the expansion of public spending in many countries. Robust domestic demand partly offset the more sluggish performance of the external sector, whose negative impact was felt more strongly in several South American countries. The fastest-growing sectors in the region were commerce, construction and financial and business services.

Investment made a smaller contribution to growth in 2012 than it had in 2011, owing mainly to the investment contraction in Argentina and Brazil, which both weigh heavily in the regional average. Investment growth was slack, too, in some Central American countries, and in Cuba and the Dominican Republic, with very low investment ratios of around 15% of GDP or less in 2012, although remittances helped to drive expansion of domestic demand. Investment was strongly up in other countries of the region, however, and Latin America and the Caribbean overall achieved an average ratio investment of 22.9% of GDP in 2012, the highest value recorded since 1981. Evidence of stronger growth in construction and commerce suggests that investment went mainly to those sectors and less to procurement of machinery and equipment.

---

[4] The two economies represent around 41.5% of the region's GDP.

Employment and wages rose, with unemployment falling more among women than among men, but there are signs that growth in "quality" employment has slowed

Employment and wages rose, with the drop in unemployment among women (0.3 percentage points as a simple average of the countries with data available) larger than among men (0.1 percentage points). For the region overall, urban unemployment eased down from 6.7% in 2011 to 6.4% in 2012, which was no small achievement in the context of a slowing global economy, but a smaller gain than in recent years: unemployment rates were 8.1% in 2009, 7.3% in 2010 and 6.7% en 2011. The drops in unemployment and rises in employment have been larger in the South American countries and have been occurring more recently in Mexico. Mexico and Central America have yet to regain pre-2009 employment levels and the Caribbean has not achieved a significant reduction in unemployment since 2009.

Higher public current spending helped to boost public sector employment in 2012, above the rate of increase of private wage employment. Other indicators suggest that improvements are still taking place in the labour market, but at a slower rate than before. Growth in formal wage employment remained strong in several countries, but slowed in Argentina and Brazil in particular, in keeping with slackening economic growth. Growth in wage employment (2.7%) in 2012 continued to outstrip growth in own-account employment (2.2%) but the difference between the two rates (which stood at 3.2% and 1.9% in 2011) narrowed. In a few countries (Argentina, the Dominican Republic and Mexico), the reverse occurred, with brisker growth in own-account employment. In most of the countries with data available (7 of 10), the services sector expanded its share in total employment, which reflects slower growth in tradable sectors, such as agriculture and industry, which are harder hit by sluggish external demand.

Generally speaking, real wages rose, which helped to bolster domestic demand, particularly consumption. Higher minimum wages in many countries contributed to the rise in real wages at the regional level. In addition, a number of countries made changes to their labour legislation, including measures to give domestic workers stronger rights and better income (Nicaragua, Uruguay and Ecuador), to broaden breastfeeding rights (Bolivarian Republic of Venezuela, Ecuador and Mexico), and to restructure social security contributions to favour labour-intensive activities (Brazil). In Mexico broader legislative changes were made, including the introduction of new types of contract and the regulation of subcontracting. Substantial changes were made in the Bolivarian Republic of Venezuela, as well, with the elimination of outsourcing, a shorter working day and a higher severance pay.

The outlook for 2013 is again for lacklustre and uncertain external conditions

The economic outlook for Latin America and the Caribbean depends heavily on how the global economy evolves in 2013. The most likely scenario is continued low growth in Europe and even recession in some European countries, although there remains a possibility that agreements will be reached that would gradually resolve the existing financial, fiscal and competitiveness imbalances. At the same time, in the wake of the presidential elections in United States, prospects have improved for a fiscal agreement, albeit a partial one, and the government has confirmed its intention to maintain an expansionary monetary policy. Some positive performance indicators are now showing in labour and housing, which together support a projection of some growth in 2013. China's rate of growth may rise —or at least should not fall— in 2013, depending on how much the country can boost domestic consumption while holding down inflation and regaining export growth. This should be aided by consolidation of a positive growth track in the United States and perhaps, though less probably, a gradual recovery (or at least a bottoming out) in Europe. This scenario also assumes that oil will not become a factor of additional instability for geopolitical reasons.

Taking this as the baseline scenario for 2013, it is estimated that GDP growth in Latin America and the Caribbean could pick up to around 3.8%, owing to two effects in particular. First, higher growth in Argentina and Brazil, on the back of recovery in the agricultural sector in Argentina and in manufacturing and investment in Brazil. An upswing in trade between the two countries could also boost their respective economic activity levels. Second, several of the region's economies are expected to experience strong domestic demand thanks to improvements in labour indicators, an increase in bank lending to the private sector and relatively stable raw material prices, since no further falls of any significance are foreseen. External demand is unlikely to make much contribution to economic growth in 2013, given the low growth context and highly uncertain external conditions.

In this scenario, growth rates should be less disparate in the region, including an uptick in the Caribbean. However, the Caribbean countries are still on a fragile fiscal footing and need fiscal reform along with external support to firmly gain sustainable fiscal consolidation paths.

In Latin America and the Caribbean, the challenge also remains of increasing and stabilizing investment growth (rather than relying solely on consumption) to drive structural change, absorb technical progress and achieve suitable growth. In this connection, tapping the regional market within an open regionalism approach could help to offset the weak rendering of external demand in the past few years.

Lastly, although it is less likely than the baseline scenario, a lower growth scenario cannot be ruled out, given the (albeit receding) possibility that external risk factors —deepening of the crisis in the eurozone, lack of agreement over how to deal with the fiscal cliff in the United States, a heavy slowdown in China or oil price hikes fuelled by political tensions in the Middle East— will worsen. In that case, the resilience the Latin American and Caribbean region has shown thus far would be more severely tested and the impact would continue to be uneven in the region, depending on the significance of each of these factors for the economies of the individual countries. A growth slowdown in the United States would affect Mexico, Central America and the Caribbean the most, whereas the other South American countries would feel the impacts more heavily if Europe remained in recession or China's economy cooled. Finally, an oil price hike could have a more or less favourable impact, depending on the countries' positions as net exporters or importers of fuels.

Chapter I

The external sector

The recession in Europe, the cooling of the Chinese economy and slow growth in the United States all contributed to a decline in global economic growth in 2012

Growth in the global economy fell slightly from 2.7% in 2011 to 2.2% in 2012. The main reason was the recession in a number of eurozone countries and its consequences for Asia and Latin America, which grew less briskly than they had in 2011, albeit still faster than the global economy as a whole. Although there were improvements in the United States and Japanese economies, these were not enough to offset the slackening performance in Europe.

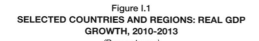

Figure I.1
SELECTED COUNTRIES AND REGIONS: REAL GDP GROWTH, 2010-2013
(Percentages)

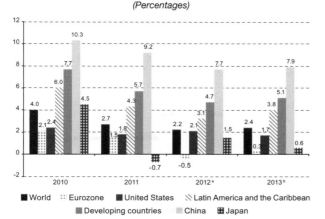

■ World ⠿ Eurozone ■ United States ╲ Latin America and the Caribbean
■ Developing countries China ▦ Japan

Source: Economic Commission for Latin America and the Caribbean (ECLAC), on the basis of United Nations, *World Economic Situation and Prospects. Mid-2012 Update,* New York, 2012.
a Estimates.
b Proyections.

The region's external conditions continued to be affected by the financial and sovereign debt crisis in some eurozone countries, the tribulations of the United States economy following the 2008-2009 crisis in its financial system, and falling growth rates in the major economies of Asia as a result of both the two factors mentioned and difficulties of their own. However, the decision by the European Central Bank (ECB) to make direct purchases of eurozone countries' sovereign debt under certain conditions, combined with the adoption of commitments to institutional change by member States, helped to reduce the likelihood of a crisis in these countries, and sovereign risk premiums came down as a result (see figure I.2).

Despite some forecasts of recession, in 2012 the United States economy showed signs of an incipient if fragile recovery, with growth of 2.1% in 2012 contrasting with the 1.8% recorded in 2011. Growth in the economies of China and India fell because of negative growth in Europe, the market for a large proportion of both countries' exports. This was compounded by the need to restructure domestic spending in China because of overinvestment in some sectors of the economy, and to reduce inflationary pressures in both countries, and by India's fiscal deficit, which left little scope for action to offset the decline in external demand.

Figure I.2
EUROPE (SELECTED COUNTRIES): RISK PREMIUMS ON FIVE-YEAR CREDIT DEFAULT SWAPS, JULY 2009 TO OCTOBER 2012
(Basis points)

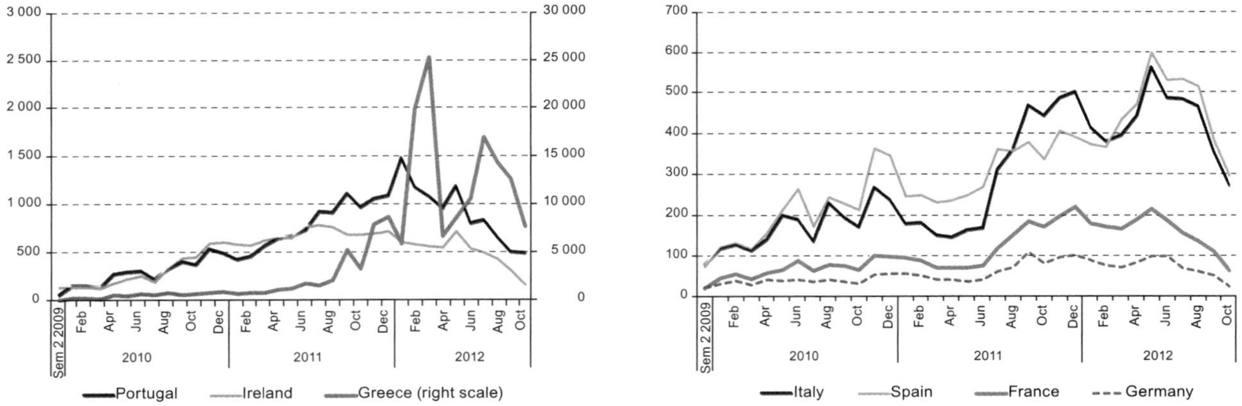

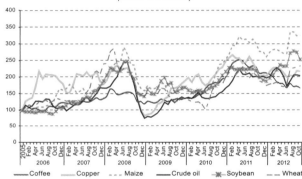

Source: Economic Commission for Latin America and the Caribbean (ECLAC), on the basis of Bloomberg figures.

In this context, price trends for the raw materials exported by Latin America and the Caribbean relative to 2011 were mixed. International prices for a number of foodstuffs began to rise in the second half of 2012 (see figure I.3). In contrast, the copper price followed a slightly downward if fluctuating trend, while the crude oil price, with some variations, tended to hold steady. In the case of oil, uncertainty increased towards the year's end as heightened geopolitical strains interfered with the normal operation of the market. At the same time, even with global liquidity still high, slow progress towards a solution to the eurozone crisis and the uncertainties surrounding the United States economy led to a slight increase in perceptions of emerging country risk, so that financial inflows to these economies fell.

Lower growth in the global economy resulted in contraction or lower growth for the region's goods and services exports

The deterioration in the world economy was transmitted to the region's economies mainly through the trade channel, owing to the fall-off in exports from Latin America and the Caribbean to Europe and China in 2012. The region's overall exports to Europe and China fell, but this decline was particularly marked in South America, including Brazil (figure I.4). Its impact on economic activity varied by the scale of exports as a proportion of each country's GDP, and by the proportion going to the European Union and China in particular. Despite the slowdown in exports to the United States market, they continued to grow faster than those to other destinations.

Figure I.3
SELECTED COMMODITY PRICE INDICES, JANUARY 2006 TO OCTOBER 2012
(Index: 2005=100)

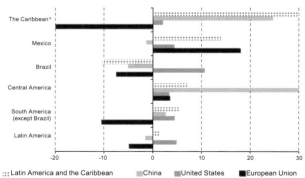

Source: Economic Commission for Latin America and the Caribbean (ECLAC), on the basis of International Monetary Fund, *Primary Commodity Prices*, November 2012.

Figure I.4
LATIN AMERICA: YEAR-ON-YEAR CHANGE IN EXPORTS, BY DESTINATION, 2011-2012 [a]
(Percentages)

Source: Economic Commission for Latin America and the Caribbean (ECLAC), on the basis of official figures.
[a] To September 2012.
[b] For the Caribbean, the data correspond to January-September (United States), January-August (European Union), January-May (China) and January-June (Latin America and the Caribbean).

Table I.1
LATIN AMERICA: EXPORT SHARES OF DESTINATION MARKETS, 2011
(Percentages)

	European Union	United States	China	Latin America and the Caribbean
Latin America	13	39	9	18
South America (except Brazil)	14	23	11	24
Central America	13	39	1	36
Brazil	21	10	17	22
Mexico	5	79	2	8

Source: Economic Commission for Latin America and the Caribbean (ECLAC), on the basis of official figures.

The export performance reduced trade flows as a share of GDP, especially in the case of exports to Europe (see table I.2). The economies of Chile, Peru and the Plurinational State of Bolivia suffered the worst effects, owing to the European market's importance as a destination for their exports and the substantial share of their GDP represented by trade flows. The impact was not so severe for Brazil, despite the sharp drop in its exports to Europe, because exports represented a smaller share of the country's GDP. Meanwhile, exports to the United States market had a particularly positive impact in GDP terms for countries exporting manufactures (such as Mexico and Costa Rica) and energy products (Ecuador and the Plurinational State of Bolivia).

Table I.2
LATIN AMERICA: ABSOLUTE GROWTH IN EXPORT VALUES AS A SHARE OF GDP, BY DESTINATION COUNTRY, SEPTEMBER 2011 TO SEPTEMBER 2012
(Percentages)

	European Union	European Union	China	Latin America and the Caribbean
Argentina	-0.4	0.0	-0.2	0.2
Bolivia (Plurinational State of)	-0.7	2.3	0.0	7.0
Brazil	-0.2	0.1	-0.1	-0.3
Chile	-1.0	0.0	-0.1	-0.5
Colombia	0.1	0.4	0.3	0.3
Costa Rica	0.9	1.5	0.2	1.9
Ecuador	-0.2	1.1	0.2	2.8
El Salvador	-0.3	-0.1	0.0	0.3
Guatemala	-0.1	-0.4	-	-
Honduras	0.0	0.2	0.2	-0.6
Mexico	0.3	1.0	0.0	0.3
Nicaragua	0.2	0.6	-0.1	1.7
Paraguay	-0.5	0.0	0.0	-0.7
Peru	-0.7	-0.3	0.2	0.2
Uruguay	-0.4	0.2	0.6	0.2
Venezuela (Bolivarian Republic of) [a]	0.0	0.1	0.0	-0.1

Source: Economic Commission for Latin America and the Caribbean (ECLAC), on the basis of official figures..
[a] Non-oil exports.

The region's exports are estimated to have risen 1.6% by value in 2012, which would represent sharply slower growth than in previous years. Falling prices for a large group of export products eroded the value exported and, by contrast with previous years, volume growth was the factor driving the modest increase in the value of exports from the South and Central American countries and Mexico (figure I.5). The exception was Brazil, where a combination of low demand from its main trading partners (the European countries and China) and a substantial drop in its intraregional trade led to a decline in export volumes.

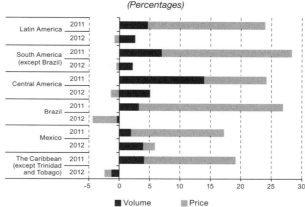

Figure I.5
LATIN AMERICA: ESTIMATED GROWTH IN EXPORT VALUES, WITH CONTRIBUTION OF VOLUMES AND PRICES, 2012
(Percentages)

Source: Economic Commission for Latin America and the Caribbean (ECLAC), on the basis of official figures.

Import prices were less variable than export prices. Volume growth appears to have been much the same for imports as for exports, but generally positive changes in the unit value of imports meant that their total value increased by more than that of exports in 2012 (see table A.6 in the statistical annex). The result is that the goods trade surplus for the region as a whole is estimated to have fallen from 1.3% of regional GDP in 2011 to 0.9% in 2012.

Over the course of 2012 a number of countries took measures to address the trade balance deterioration (see table I.3). Argentina and Brazil stand out, as the measures taken there had a large impact on trade flows within the region because of the large share of intraregional trade these two countries represent.

Table I.3
LATIN AMERICA (SELECTED COUNTRIES AND MERCOSUR): TRADE MEASURES, 2012

Country	Measure	Date implemented
Argentina	All merchandise imports require an import affidavit in advance. The administrative process delays imports, and an import licence may be refused in some cases.	February 2012
	Unwinding of the free trade regime between MERCOSUR and Mexico for motor vehicles: implementation of a 35% tariff on automobiles from Mexico and a tariff of between 16% and 18% on auto parts.	June 2012
	Requirement that importers balance imports with exports unless they increase the local content of the products they manufacture in Argentina, or alternatively that they not transfer revenues abroad.	July 2012
	Imposition of a 14% tariff on imports of capital goods from outside MERCOSUR. Tariff of 2% on capital goods produced outside the country.	July 2012
Brazil	Brazil and Mexico agree to a temporary review of the motor vehicle free trade agreement, under which light vehicles can be imported tariff-free only up to certain gradually rising ceilings.	March 2012
	Termination of the system of automatic import licensing for several categories of perishable goods imports from Argentina.	May 2012
Colombia	Entry into effect of free trade agreement with the United States.	May 2012
Ecuador	Imposition of trade restrictions on imports of 627 tariff items from all over the world.	January 2012
MERCOSUR	Authorization for member countries to increase import tax rates above the common external tariff for a maximum of 100 tariff positions for up to 12 months, with the possibility of an extension for up to a further 12 months. In June 2012, this measure was extended to a maximum of 200 tariff positions.	January 2012
Mexico	Introduction of tariffs on automobiles (20%) and auto parts (from 0% to 20%) from Argentina.	June 2012

Source: Economic Commission for Latin America and the Caribbean (ECLAC), on the basis of official information from the countries concerned.

The services balance also continued to deteriorate in 2012 (see figure I.10). One of the main reasons appears to have been the increased cost of freight, insurance and other services associated with goods imports (whose volume continued to increase, as noted above). The most negative outcome was in South America. By contrast, the services balance held steady as a share of GDP in the Central American countries and Mexico.

International tourism is a major source of revenue, particularly in the Caribbean and Central America. Tourist arrivals increased, but did not reach the levels seen before the 2008 crisis (see figure I.6). This is explained by weak economic growth in the United States and Europe, the main source countries for tourists to both subregions. These effects were also felt in Mexico, the region's largest tourist destination. Tourism in South America began to trend downward in 2011, and this trend continued in 2012. This partly reflected the slowdown in the region's economies, which affected intraregional tourism and international business travel, both major sources of inbound tourism in the South American countries.

Figure I.6
LATIN AMERICA AND THE CARIBBEAN: YEAR-ON-YEAR GROWTH IN INTERNATIONAL TOURIST ARRIVALS, JANUARY 2009 TO AUGUST 2012
(Percentages, three-month moving averages)

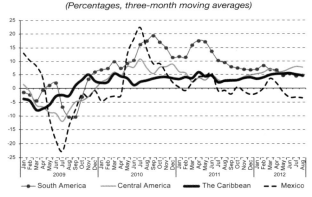

Source: Economic Commission for Latin America and the Caribbean (ECLAC), on the basis of figures from the World Tourism Organization (UNWTO).

Weaker external demand resulted in a slight worsening of the terms of trade

As a result of lower global economic growth, especially in Europe and, to a lesser degree, in Asia, prices for some commodities that account for a large share of the region's export basket trended downward in 2012 (see figure I.7). Food prices were a partial exception to this trend, as they did not decline but rather fluctuated as a consequence of climatic factors. Prices fell during the first half of the year, particularly for sugar and wheat, but in the third quarter there was an upturn driven by higher prices for cereals (maize, wheat and rice). One factor was the drought that hit farm production in the United States, and this contributed to a pick-up in inflation in Latin America and the Caribbean, particularly in the net food-importing countries of Central America and the Caribbean. In the tropical beverages category, coffee and cacao prices fell heavily, mainly as a result of rising global output. Prices for vegetable oils and oilseeds rose substantially during 2012 because of poor weather conditions resulting in a smaller than expected soybean harvest in Argentina, Paraguay and Brazil.

Figure I.7
**LATIN AMERICA: PRICE INDICES FOR EXPORT COMMODITIES AND MANUFACTURES,
JANUARY 2008 TO OCTOBER 2012 [a]**
(Index: 2000=100, three-month moving average)

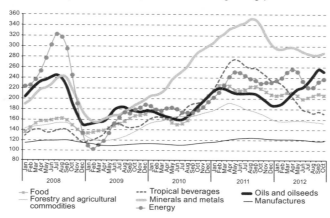

Food
Forestry and agricultural commodities
Tropical beverages
Minerals and metals
Energy
Oils and oilseeds
Manufactures

Source: Economic Commission for Latin America and the Caribbean (ECLAC), on the basis of figures from the United Nations Conference on Trade and Development (UNCTAD) and the Netherlands Bureau of Economic Policy Analysis (CPB).
[a] The export commodity groups are weighted by their share of Latin American exports.

Lower demand from emerging and developing economies, particularly in Asia, led to a drop in metal and mineral prices. The price of copper, one of the Peru's and especially Chile's main exports, was far below its 2011 level, while the prices of nickel, tin, lead and zinc also fell short of the year before. The price of iron, Brazil's main commodity export and the region's second-largest after copper, was among those that fell most in 2012. The only metal whose price increased was gold, a major export item for Peru.

After remaining high in the early months of 2012, the oil price fell back in the second quarter. This tendency was reversed in the third quarter, however, when it came very close to its 2011 level. The oil prices limited movement reflects both a rise in global production (particularly in the Middle East) and a slackening of demand, especially in the eurozone.

Given these developments, the region's terms of trade are estimated to have fallen by 2.2% in 2012 (see figure I.8). For South America, however, a 3.5% decline is estimated, with exporters of mining and metal products (Chile, Peru and Brazil) suffering the largest downturn, while the other countries in the region saw modest terms-of-trade gains. Hydrocarbon-exporting countries (the Bolivarian Republic of Venezuela, Ecuador and the Plurinational State of Bolivia) are estimated to have experienced a moderate upturn in their terms of trade because of high oil prices in the first quarter of the year and the reversal of the downward trend of the second quarter. Countries exporting agro-industrial products (Argentina, Paraguay and Uruguay) are also estimated to have seen an improvement, chiefly owing to higher prices for cereals and oilseeds following the drop in production caused by poor weather conditions.

Terms of trade are estimated to have declined by 1.7% for the Central American countries and 3.2% for the Caribbean countries. The deterioration is attributable to the fall in the prices of the main products exported by these subregions (sugar, coffee and metals). In the case of Mexico, terms of trade improved slightly owing to the fact that its main exports are manufactures.

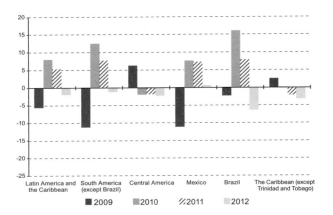

Figure I.8
LATIN AMERICA: ESTIMATED CHANGE IN TERMS OF TRADE, 2009-2012 [a]
(Percentages)

Source: Economic Commission for Latin America and the Caribbean (ECLAC), on the basis of official figures.
[a] Data for 2012 are estimates.

While profit remittances fell, worker remittances rose to varying degrees

In 2012, the factor income deficit is estimated to have improved slightly in nominal terms, to 2.3% of regional GDP, reversing the downward trend of recent years. This development is linked to the decline in a number of export commodity prices in 2012, resulting in lower earnings for foreign firms operating or investing in the region, with the consequent decline in profit remittances. Brazil, Chile, Colombia and Mexico were the countries reporting the largest outflows in absolute terms. However, three of these (Brazil, Chile and Mexico) recorded a drop in net outflows (of 34%, 15% and 1%, respectively),[1] while Colombia experienced a rise of 14%[2] because of greater outflows associated with foreign direct investment (FDI), mainly in the oil sector.

Current transfers, consisting mainly of remittances from workers abroad, rose slightly. Their share of GDP held steady at 1.1% in 2012, albeit with large variations from country to country (see figure I.9). The significant increases in El Salvador and Guatemala were due to a relative upturn in economic activity and labour market prospects in the United States, while the rise in Nicaragua

was chiefly due to the work of the country's migrants in Costa Rica. The declines in remittance flows to Colombia and Ecuador, meanwhile, reflected the difficult employment situation in Spain, the main destination for Colombian and Ecuadorian migrants, where unemployment stood at around 25%.

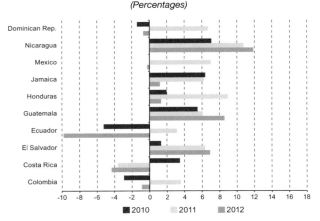

Figure I.9
LATIN AMERICA AND THE CARIBBEAN (10 COUNTRIES): YEAR-ON-YEAR CHANGE IN EMIGRANT WORKERS' REMITTANCES, 2010-2012 [a]
(Percentages)

Source: Economic Commission for Latin America and the Caribbean (ECLAC), on the basis of official figures.
[a] The rates for 2012 are calculated on the basis of data available up to the second quarter (up to the third quarter in the cases of El Salvador, Guatemala, Jamaica, Mexico and Nicaragua).

The balance-of-payments current account is estimated to have worsened in most of the region's countries

Chiefly as a consequence of the deteriorating trade balance, it is estimated that the Latin American countries posted a balance-of-payments current account deficit equivalent to 1.6% of regional GDP in 2012, a slight deterioration from the 1.3% in 2011. Because of the cooling world economy, the value of exports is estimated to have grown by less (2%) than that of imports (4%), with the trade balance thus deteriorating from a surplus of 0.1% of GDP in 2011 to a deficit of 0.4% in 2012. The surplus on the current transfers account, meanwhile, is estimated to have held steady at 1.1% of GDP. The income account deficit is estimated to have narrowed slightly from 2.5% to 2.3% of GDP (see figure I.10).

---

[1]   Data up to the third quarter.
[2]   Data up to the second quarter.

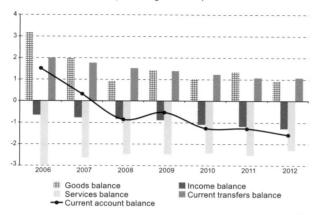

Figure I.10
LATIN AMERICA: STRUCTURE OF THE CURRENT ACCOUNT, 2006-2012 [a]
(Percentages of GDP)

- Goods balance
- Services balance
- Income balance
- Current transfers balance
- Current account balance

Source: Economic Commission for Latin America and the Caribbean (ECLAC), on the basis of official figures.
[a] Data for 2012 are estimates.

For the South American countries as a group, the current account deficit is estimated to have risen from 1.1% to 1.5% of GDP, chiefly owing to a decline in their goods trade surplus resulting from lower demand for commodities and a terms-of-trade deterioration, particularly for the countries exporting most to the eurozone and China. There were large differences between the region's countries in this respect, however. Chile and Peru appear to have seen a considerably smaller goods trade surplus because of declining exports to Asia and Europe. Brazil's trade deficit is estimated to have risen, as exports fell heavily. By contrast, goods balances appear to have improved in Ecuador and the Plurinational Sate of Bolivia, owing to higher hydrocarbon prices and an increase in export volumes. Mexico's trade balance is estimated to have held fairly steady as a proportion of GDP, although its current account deficit narrowed as a result of lower factor income outflows. Central America's current account deficit also appears to have remained fairly unchanged at about 7% of GDP.

Table I.4
LATIN AMERICA: CURRENT ACCOUNT STRUCTURE BY SUBREGION, 2011-2012 [a]
(Percentages of GDP)

	Goods balance		Services balance		Income balance		Transfers balance		Current account	
	2011	2012	2011	2012	2011	2012	2011	2012	2011	2012
Latin America	1.3	0.9	-1.2	-1.3	-2.5	-2.3	1.1	1.1	-1.3	-1.6
South America	2.7	2.2	-1.5	-1.6	-2.7	-2.5	0.4	0.4	-1.1	-1.5
Central America	-16.1	-15.5	3.7	3.8	-3.4	-3.6	8.7	8.3	-7.1	-7.0
Mexico	-0.1	0.0	-1.2	-1.2	-1.5	-1.4	2.0	1.9	-0.8	-0.7

Source: Economic Commission for Latin America and the Caribbean (ECLAC), on the basis of official figures.
[a] Data for 2012 are estimates.

Global financial uncertainty and smaller issues of sovereign bonds reduced net short-term capital inflows

Financial flows into the region continued to exceed the current account deficit and refinancing needs, so that international reserves tended to continue to build up (see table I.5), but there were changes from 2011. In the first place, net financial inflows were significantly down on the previous year and this, in combination with a larger current account deficit, meant that the reserves build-up was only 50% of that seen in 2011. This smaller inflow of foreign exchange helped to relieve the pressure for nominal currency appreciation in a number of economies. In some countries, this was a deliberate goal which the authorities pursued by imposing reserve requirements or taxes on capital inflows, or by issuing fewer sovereign bonds abroad.

In the second place, the drop in net inflows was mainly accounted for by increased outflows in the other net investment liabilities category, which includes the most volatile and shortest-dated components of external financing, and whose evolution partly reflected increased uncertainty in global financial markets. The greatest outflows were from Argentina, the Bolivarian Republic of Venezuela and Mexico, but those from Chile, Colombia, Costa Rica, Guatemala and Uruguay were also substantial.

Table I.5
LATIN AMERICA (SELECTED COUNTRIES): ESTIMATED BALANCE-OF-PAYMENTS COMPONENTS [a]
(Millions of dollars)

	Current account balance			Capital, financial and errors and omissions account			Reserves and related items		
	2010	2011	2012 [b]	2010	2011	2012 [b]	2010	2011	2012 [b]
Argentina	2 791	-307	1 487	1 367	-5 801	-2 721	-4 157	6 108	1 234
Bolivia (Plurinational State of)	969	537	1 180	-46	1 623	434	-923	-2 160	-1 614
Brazil	-47 272	-52 481	-54 087	96 373	111 118	76 451	-49 101	-58 637	-22 364
Chile	3 269	-3 220	-6 064	-245	17 410	3 387	-3 024	-14 190	2 677
Colombia	-8 758	-10 032	-11 836	11 893	13 776	15 793	-3 136	-3 744	-3 957
Costa Rica	-1 281	-2 185	-2 383	1 842	2 318	2 843	-561	-132	-460
Ecuador	-1 625	-238	-427	413	510	1 905	1 212	-272	-1 479
El Salvador	-576	-1 070	-1 150	281	656	1 132	295	414	18
Guatemala	-626	-1 456	-1 781	1 303	1 661	1 685	-677	-206	95
Honduras	-955	-1 503	-1 623	1 523	1 560	1 226	-569	-57	397
Mexico	-4 456	-11 073	-7 860	25 071	39 253	24 184	-20 615	-28 180	-16 323
Panama	-2 862	-3 874	-4 260	3 313	3 527	3 908	-452	347	352
Paraguay	-654	-270	-469	973	1 054	510	-319	-784	-41
Peru	-3 782	-3 341	-6 133	14 973	8 066	18 371	-11 191	-4 725	-12 238
Uruguay	-739	-1 324	-1 399	378	3 888	3 973	361	-2 564	-2 574
Venezuela (Bolivarian Republic of)	12 071	24 615	15 958	-20 131	-28 647	-20 241	8 060	4 032	4 283
Latin America	**-54 487**	**-67 222**	**-80 847**	**139 284**	**171 973**	**132 843**	**-84 797**	**-104 751**	**-51 995**

Source: Economic Commission for Latin America and the Caribbean (ECLAC), on the basis of official figures.
[a] The countries in this table have published quarterly balance-of-payments information up to June 2012 and, in the cases of the Bolivarian Republic of Venezuela, Brazil, Chile, Mexico and Peru, up to and including September.
[b] Estimates.

Third, while net FDI diminished slightly, it remained substantially above 2010 levels, reflecting the region's attractiveness as an investment destination. Lastly, net portfolio investment showed a slight increase over 2011, especially in Mexico.[3] Generally speaking, private-sector bond issues abroad were highly dynamic in 2012, exceeding sovereign issues (which fell in the case of countries such as Bolivarian Republic of Venezuela, El Salvador, the Dominican Republic and Mexico), despite a small increase in risk in the region (see figure I.11 and table A.14 in the statistical annex).

---

[3] The substantial shifts in flows of net portfolio investment and other net investment liabilities in the case of Mexico were due to a reorientation of its public borrowing strategy. As with other countries in earlier years, preference was given to debt issuance in the local market, reducing exposure to foreign currency-denominated external debt. This translated into a rise in portfolio investment as local bonds were purchased by non-residents. If these resources are used to pay off external borrowings, outflows in the other investment liabilities category increase. The two movements tend to offset each other, albeit not completely if overall debt increases at the same time.

Figure I.11
LATIN AMERICA: EXTERNAL BOND ISSUES AND COUNTRY RISK, JANUARY 2007 TO OCTOBER 2012
(Millions of dollars and basis points)

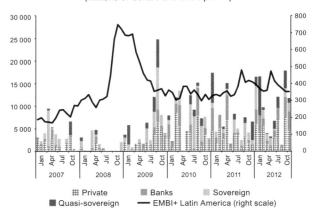

Source: Economic Commission for Latin America and the Caribbean (ECLAC), on the basis of figures from LatinFinance (bonds database), JP Morgan and Merrill Lynch.

Table I.6
LATIN AMERICA (SELECTED COUNTRIES): ESTIMATED FINANCIAL ACCOUNT COMPONENTS, 2010-2012 [a]
(Millions of dollars)

	Financial account balance			Net foreign direct investment			Net portfolio investment and other net investment liabilities		
	2010	2011	2012[b]	2010	2011	2012[b]	2010	2011	2012[b]
Argentina	2 273	-886	-736	6 090	7 183	6 401	-3 817	-8 069	-7 137
Bolivia (Plurinational State of)	924	1 522	1 554	672	859	525	252	663	1 029
Brazil	98 792	110 817	78 613	36 917	67 690	66 137	61 875	43 127	12 476
Chile	-5 927	18 118	4 044	6 142	5 477	4 864	-12 069	12 641	-820
Colombia	11 768	13 494	13 952	184	5 546	13 771	11 584	7 948	181
Costa Rica	1 933	2 536	1 807	1 441	2 099	2 200	492	437	-393
Ecuador	235	360	1 229	161	640	578	73	-280	651
El Salvador	-607	916	3 414	117	385	258	-723	530	3 156
Guatemala	1 584	2 002	815	782	967	1 054	802	1 035	-249
Honduras	1 419	1 534	1 499	971	997	1 059	448	537	440
Mexico	44 070	40 716	33 084	5 911	8 685	-4 730	38 159	32 031	37 814
Panama	2 908	4 224	1 957	2 350	2 790	2 823	557	1 434	-866
Paraguay	457	836	260	340	483	239	118	353	21
Peru	12 480	9 161	19 884	7 062	8 119	9 641	5 418	1 042	10 243
Uruguay	1 085	4 256	3 093	2 349	2 629	2 768	-1 263	1 627	325
Venezuela (Bolivarian Republic of)	-17 762	-24 818	-17 685	-1 462	4 875	-759	-16 300	-29 693	-16 926
Latin America	**155 632**	**184 787**	**146 784**	**70 027**	**119 424**	**106 839**	**85 605**	**65 363**	**39 945**

Source: Economic Commission for Latin America and the Caribbean (ECLAC), on the basis of official figures.
[a] The countries in this table have published quarterly balance-of-payments information up to June 2012 and, in the cases of the Bolivarian Republic of Venezuela, Brazil, Chile, Mexico and Peru, up to and including September.
[b] Estimates.

Chapter II

Fiscal and monetary variables

The fiscal position deteriorated, especially in the Caribbean

In 2012, the fiscal balances of the region's countries deteriorated relative to 2011, mainly because of public spending growth. In Latin America, primary balances (before interest payments on the public debt) averaged a deficit of 0.3 percentage points of GDP, as compared to a surplus of 0.2 percentage points in 2011, while overall balances (including interest payments) yielded a negative result of 2 percentage points of regional GDP (see table II.1 and the statistical annex).

Table II.1
LATIN AMERICA AND THE CARIBBEAN: CENTRAL GOVERNMENT FISCAL INDICATORS, FISCAL BALANCE 2012 AND ESTIMATED CHANGES IN REVENUES AND SPENDING, 2011-2012 [a]
(Percentages of GDP)

Region/country	Overall balance 2012	Primary balance 2012	Changes estimated between 2011 and 2012								
					Breakdown of spending				Breakdown of revenues		
			Overall balance	Total spending [b]	Primary current spending	Interest	Capital spending	Total revenues	Tax revenues [c]	Income from non-renewable products [c]	Other income
Latin America and the Caribbean (32 countries)	-2.8	-0.4	-0.4	0.7	0.5	0.0	0.3	0.3	0.3	...	0.0
Latin America (19 countries)	-2.0	-0.3	-0.4	1.0	0.7	0.0	0.5	0.6	0.6	...	0.0
The Caribbean (13 countries)	-4.0	-0.5	-0.4	0.3	0.2	0.0	0.1	0.0	-0.1	...	0.1
Central America and the Dominican Republic	-2.7	-0.8	-0.3	0.7	0.4	0.0	0.3	0.4	0.3	...	0.1
Hydrocarbon exporters [d]	-2.5	-0.6	-0.4	0.8	-0.1	0.1	1.1	0.5	0.7	-0.1	-0.2
Mineral and metal exporters [e]	0.3	1.1	-0.8	0.8	0.8	0.0	0.0	0.0	0.5	-0.6	0.1
Food exporters [f]	-2.2	-0.6	-1.5	2.5	2.3	-0.1	0.3	1.0	0.8	...	0.2
Services exporters [g]	-4.1	-0.1	-0.1	-0.1	0.0	0.1	-0.1	-0.2	0.1	...	-0.3
Brazil	-2.2	1.8	0.4	0.2	...	-0.9	...	0.6	0.6	...	0.0
Mexico	-2.4	-0.6	0.1	0.6	0.1	0.0	0.6	0.8	1.1	0.1	-0.4

Source: Economic Commission for Latin America and the Caribbean (ECLAC), on the basis of official estimates.
[a] The data for 2012 are estimates.
[b] The variation in total spending includes changes in net lending.
[c] Income from non-renewable products includes tax income from the exploitation of non-renewable natural resources.
[d] Bolivarian Republic of Venezuela, Colombia, Ecuador, Plurinational State of Bolivia, and Trinidad and Tobago.
[e] Chile and Peru.
[f] Argentina, Paraguay and Uruguay.
[g] Antigua and Barbuda, Bahamas, Barbados, Belize, Dominica, Granada, Jamaica, Panama, Saint Kitts and Nevis, Saint Vincent and the Grenadines and Saint Lucia.

The average performance of the fiscal accounts in 2012 was the outcome of an increase of 1 percentage point of GDP in fiscal revenues combined with a rise of 1.5 GDP percentage points in public spending (see figure II.1). Spending increases outstripped revenue growth in several countries, and overall results worsened accordingly.

Figure II.1
LATIN AMERICA (19 COUNTRIES): CENTRAL GOVERNMENT FISCAL INDICATORS, 2000-2012 [a]
(Percentages of GDP)

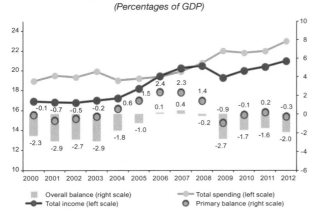

Source: Economic Commission for Latin America and the Caribbean (ECLAC), on the basis of official figures.
[a] Simple averages. The data for 2012 are estimates.

The average fiscal balance in the region was well down on the level achieved before the crisis. In 2012, nine countries recorded primary surpluses (47% of the total), whereas in 2003-2008 the balance had been positive in 15 countries (almost 80% of the total). Despite the deterioration in the fiscal positions, the average debt-to-GDP ratio for 19 countries of Latin America is estimated to have continued on its downward path, falling from 30.5% of GDP in 2011 to 29.6% in 2012 at the central government level (see the statistical annex). In some cases the gross public debt data are official budgetary projections, while in others they are the latest figures available, so that this indicator is likely to have risen by year's end, especially in countries with large deficits (public debt is expected to have increased sharply in the Dominican Republic over the latter months of 2012, for example).

The hydrocarbon-exporting countries, which obtain between 20% and 40% of their fiscal revenues from these resources, saw their fiscal deficits widen, on average, as heavy capital spending outweighed higher income. With the exception of Colombia and the Plurinational State of Bolivia, where fiscal revenues from hydrocarbons rose faster than GDP, in this group of countries oil income either held fairly steady (Mexico) or fell considerably (the Bolivarian Republic of Venezuela, Ecuador, and Trinidad and Tobago).

The deterioration in the fiscal balance in the mineral- and metal-exporting countries, Chile and Peru, reflected a rise in current spending and a contraction in mining resources that was offset by the upswing in non-mining tax revenues. Food-exporting countries posted a heavy increase in current spending, together with a smaller increase in fiscal income (particularly tax revenues). In Argentina revenues rose faster than expenditures.

Although the average figures for Central America show the fiscal accounts deteriorating, the deficit is especially wide in the Dominican Republic, at 6.8% of GDP, and in Costa Rica, at 4.5%. By contrast, in Guatemala and, especially, in El Salvador the overall balance improved significantly, while Nicaragua has been running a surplus since 2011.

The Caribbean countries continued to record high public borrowing and deficit levels. In previous years, raw material-dependent countries such as Belize, Guyana, Suriname and Trinidad and Tobago had sustained a better financial and fiscal performance, but this deteriorated sharply in 2012. Service economies such as Antigua and Barbuda, the Bahamas, Barbados and Jamaica have been badly affected by the drop in revenues from tourism and offshore financial services since the start of the international financial crisis and continued feel these effects in 2012. Thus, public debt in Barbados and Jamaica rose to 106% and 128% of GDP, respectively, in 2012.

The large fiscal deficits in the services-exporting economies of the Caribbean continued to widen in 2012, as revenues, especially from grants, shrank. Tax income declined (except in Saint Kitts and Nevis, Saint Vincent and the Grenadines, and Saint Lucia), as contractions in these countries' main trading partners dragged on economic growth. Bahamas, Barbados and Dominica posted high rates of public investment, and Panama yielded a steadily rising fiscal deficit owing to heavy capital expenditures in the past few years.

The performance observed in Latin America was the outcome of disparate tendencies (see figure II.2), as the fiscal accounts improved in eight countries (Argentina, Bolivarian Republic of Venezuela, Brazil, Colombia, El Salvador, Guatemala, Mexico and the Plurinational State of Bolivia), and the overall balance deteriorated in nine (Chile, Costa Rica, the Dominican Republic, Ecuador, Nicaragua, Panama, Paraguay, Peru and Uruguay) (see table II.1). The South American countries and Mexico, which are the most dependent on non-tax resources, were able to keep their public deficits at moderate levels since the deterioration in natural resource prices was gradual, and as a result were able to control borrowing as a percentage of GDP.

The estimates show that most of the countries still had a slightly negative GDP gap in 2012 (as a result of the recovery from the international financial crisis). Fiscal policies have not been clearly countercyclical as they were in 2009, although the larger deficits coincide with negative GDP gaps in some countries (see figure II.2). As discussed in *Economic Survey of Latin America and the Caribbean 2012* (pp. 41-42) most of the region's countries, with the exception of some Central American and Caribbean countries, are on a footing to implement more active countercyclical policies should external conditions worsen. The low public debt levels should, in coordination with monetary policy, permit sufficient fiscal space to offset temporary falls in aggregate demand. The GDP gap remained negative for all the Caribbean countries in 2012, and widening deficits have reduced their fiscal capacity still further.

Figure II.2
LATIN AMERICA (22 COUNTRIES): CENTRAL GOVERNMENT FISCAL POSITION, 2011-2012 [a]
(Percentages of GDP)

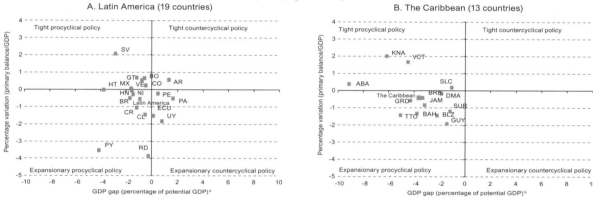

Source: Economic Commission for Latin America and the Caribbean (ECLAC), on the basis of official figures.
[a] Simple averages. Data for 2012 are estimates. Data for Barbados, Mexico, Panama and the Plurinational State of Bolivia refer to the non-financial public sector; those for Saint Kitts and Nevis to the federal government.
[b] GDP gap = (actual GDP - trend GDP)*100/(Trend GDP).

The decline in non-tax resources was offset by higher tax revenues

With the global economy slowing and the terms of trade gradually deteriorating, income from the exploitation of natural resources or commodities was stood still or fell in 2012 relative to the buoyant performance of the year before, although in many of the region's countries fiscal revenues of this type still make up a substantial share of the total (see figure II.3). Tax revenues were more dynamic, however, which may be attributed to domestic demand, with some countries' private-sector consumption and investment rising considerably, especially in the construction sector.

In countries where revenues increased (13 of 19), the rise was usually quite moderate (see figure II.4). It exceeded 1% of GDP only in Argentina (1.6%), Ecuador (1.6%), El Salvador (1.3%), Panama (1.1%), Paraguay (1.7%) and the Plurinational State of Bolivia (5.5%), while the largest fall was in the Bolivarian Republic of Venezuela, with a decline of 3.6% of output. The increase in the tax burden in Argentina (by 1.5% of GDP) was accounted for mainly by domestic consumption, growth in exports of seeds, oil crops and mineral fuels (with both prices and volumes up) and a rise in taxable incomes and registered employment. Fiscal revenue growth in the Plurinational State of Bolivia was essentially down to higher revenues from hydrocarbons and a broadening of the tax base. Meanwhile, the various tax measures or reforms being pursued in many countries (Argentina, Chile, the Dominican Republic, Ecuador, El Salvador, Guatemala, Panama and Peru) will, increase the tax burden in coming years (see table II.2).

Figure II.3
LATIN AMERICA AND THE CARIBBEAN: TOTAL FISCAL REVENUE AND TAX REVENUE, 2005-2012
(Percentages)

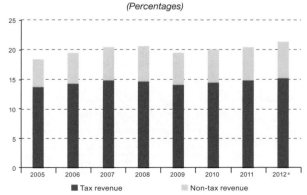

Source: Economic Commission for Latin America and the Caribbean (ECLAC), on the basis of official figures.
[a] Estimates.

Figure II.4
LATIN AMERICA AND THE CARIBBEAN (SELECTED COUNTRIES): CHANGE IN CENTRAL GOVERNMENT REVENUE AND EXPENDITURE, 2011-2012 [a]
(Percentages of GDP)

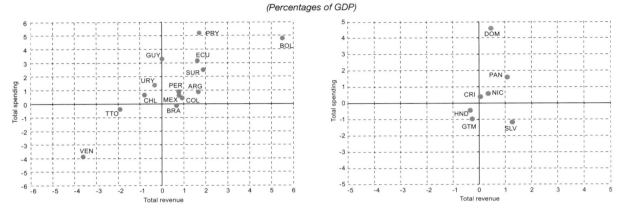

Source: Economic Commission for Latin America and the Caribbean (ECLAC), on the basis of official figures.
[a] The data for 2012 are estimates.

Table II.2
LATIN AMERICA AND THE CARIBBEAN: PUBLIC FINANCE MEASURES AND REFORMS, 2012

Country	Reform
Argentina	(i) Expropriation of YPF: a law was enacted decreeing the expropriation of 51% of YPF shares and declaring the attainment of self-sufficiency in hydrocarbons and their exploitation, industrialization, transportation and commercialization to be "priority objectives" that were "in the public interest".
	(ii) Charter of the Central Bank of Argentina: the Argentine Congress approved the new central bank charter. Article 20 of the charter establishes that the bank may make temporary advances to the national government up to an amount equivalent to 12% of the monetary base. It may also make advances not exceeding 10% of the cash resources the national government has raised in the past 12 months. Exceptionally, and if the situation or prospects of the national or international economy warrant this, it may temporarily advance an additional sum not exceeding the equivalent of 10% of the cash resources the national government has raised in the past 12 months. This exceptional faculty may be exercised for a period not exceeding 18 months.
	(iii) Measures to control capital outflows, such as a 15% surcharge on acquisitions of goods and leasing or provision of services abroad by persons resident in Argentina using credit, store or debit cards or carried out over the Internet in commercial establishments abroad, and a ban on the purchase of dollars with the use of peso-denominated mortgages for real estate purchases.
	(iv) On the current expenditure side, there was particularly strong growth in social security benefits, mainly because of the effects of applying the social security benefit portability policy, increases in pensions for the armed forces and security forces and upward revisions to benefits in compliance with court injunctions. Spending on pay also rose, essentially because a number of collective agreements reached during 2011 and the first two quarters of 2012 with a view to improving the purchasing power of national public-sector workers came into full effect.
Brazil	As part of the Brasil Maior programme, the goal of which is to increase industrial competitiveness, 15 labour-intensive sectors benefited in August from the replacement of social contributions by a 1% or 2% tax on gross incomes. There was also a reduction in petrol and diesel taxes and in the industrial products tax (applied to vehicles, trucks, construction equipment, household electrical appliances, furniture, wallpaper, etc.); accelerated depreciation was applied for payment of the Contribution for the Financing of Social Security (COFINS) (Social Integration Programme – PIS/PASEP) on capital goods purchases; the cash limits for application of the reduced taxes of the Integrated System for Payment of Microenterprise Taxes (SIMPLE) and the Individual Microenterprise Programme (MEI) were raised; the reimbursement regime for exporters was changed; and financial operations taxes (IOF) on lending to individuals were cut from 3% to 1.5%.
	On the expenditure side, a key development was the introduction of the Growth Acceleration Programme (PAC) for vehicle and equipment purchases. In addition, personnel expenditure and social charges increased owing to a reallocation of commission expenditure to personnel expenditure, competitive recruitment of new government personnel and pay increases, all of which also resulted in a rise in social security expenditure. There was an increase in extraordinary credits for the north-eastern region, which had suffered a long drought. Lastly, interest payment subsidies were increased for the rural and agro-industrial sector and farming families, as were subsidies to the National Bank for Economic and Social Development (BNDES) for financing operations, and debt forgiveness was granted in the rural sector, together with compensation and reinstatement in the Agricultural Activity Guarantee Programme (PROAGRO).
Chile	The Tax Legislation Improvement Act, which comes into force on 1 January 2013, increases the corporation tax rate to 20%, harmonizes transfer price rules, increases and alters the composition of the cigarette tax, reduces the top annual rate of stamp duty from 0.6% to 0.4%, lowers marginal rates for employee income tax (*impuesto único de segunda categoría*) and supplementary personal income tax (*impuesto global complementario*) in all brackets, except for taxpayers in the highest bracket, and provides a tax credit for families with monthly incomes not exceeding 66 development units (UF) to deduct education expenditure, up to a limit of 100,000 pesos per child.
Costa Rica	In December 2011, the Legislative Assembly of Costa Rica decreed the Legal Entities Taxation Act, under which all corporations shall pay a sum of between 25% and 50% of one monthly basic wage.
	In September 2012, the Legislative Assembly put into effect the Strengthening of Tax Administration Act and the Enforcement of the Fiscal Transparency Standard Act.
Dominican Republic	On 10 November 2012, the executive enacted the Strengthening the Tax-raising Capacity of the State for Fiscal Sustainability and Sustainable Development Act No. 253-12, which makes changes to income taxes (ISR) and the goods and services transfer tax (ITBIS), creates new asset and income taxes and amends incentive laws, among other things. These measures will come into effect on 1 January 2013. The new ITBIS brackets will come into force on the same date and the actual tax take from them will be known from February. The general ITBIS rate is raised from 16% to 18% and a 1% tax on the total real estate assets of physical persons is established.
Ecuador	Recent amendments to tax law include, for financial institutions, the reversal of the rate reduction for income tax payable on sums reinvested in production assets, a change in the way minimum advance payments of that tax are calculated, the introduction of value added tax (VAT) on financial services, the establishment of exceptions to banking confidentiality and an increase in the foreign assets tax rate.
	The Social Spending Redistribution Act was published in November 2012, its purpose being to generate resources that will help to finance an increase in the Human Development Bond. In particular, VAT will now apply to financial services and there will be increases in the rate of income tax (from 13% to 23%) and the foreign assets tax.
	Reforms to the Regulations for the Application of the Currency Remittance Tax and the Regulations for the Application of the Internal Tax Regime Act came into force in June 2012.

Table II.2 (concluded)

Country	Reform
El Salvador	(i) Tax reform: the tax reform passed by the Legislative Assembly in late 2011 came into force during the 2012 fiscal year. Its main provisions include: an increase from 25% to 30% in the top rate of corporation tax, applicable to firms with annual earnings of over US$ 150,000; the introduction of a minimum tax of 1% of gross revenues for firms reporting two consecutive years of losses; a rise from 1.5% to 1.75% in the monthly payment on account for corporate and personal income tax; and a reduction from 10% to 5% in the tax on dividends paid or credited. (ii) The Results-based Budgeting with a Gender Perspective pilot operation: the 2012 State General Budget Act provides for pilot trials of results-based budgeting with a gender perspective in the Ministries of Health, Agriculture and Livestock, Education, and Environment and Natural Resources. These pilots include goals and tracking indicators for the main programmes and projects, and their aim is to create an explicit link between progress in attaining these goals and the resources allocated. (iii) The 2012 public-sector saving and austerity policy: in April 2012, under Decree No. 78, the Office of the President of the Republic brought in a number of measures to control government spending, including restrictions on new recruitment and a reduction of 10% in allocations for central government goods and services procurement.
Guatemala	The second Anti-evasion Act was passed in January 2012 and the Tax Modernization Act in February. Among the main measures provided for by these laws are a gradual reduction from 2013 in the corporation tax rate (from 31% to 25%), together with greater controls on deductible costs and expenditure; a 5% rate for dividends, which were formerly exempt; a gradual increase in the simplified tax regime rate; a reduction in the rates applicable to wage employees; a specific tax on first-time motor vehicle registration; and an increase in the vehicle road tax.
Mexico	The main tax measure was the abolition of the tax on vehicle ownership or use. In April 2012, personal taxpayers could deduct their spending on school fees during the 2011 fiscal year, which affected the tax take by a sum estimated at 13.554 billion pesos. On the expenditure side, subsidies provided under the following programmes increased: People's Health Insurance (SPS); the Oportunidades human development programme; Medical Insurance for a New Generation; Care for Families and the Vulnerable Population and Health Caravans; the Federal Housing Financing and Subsidy Scheme; Basic Infrastructure for Indigenous Peoples (PIBAI); the Agricultural Insurance Premium Subsidy; Indigenous School Hostels; Improvement of the Fiscal Coordination System; Transfers to the Social Support Fund for Mexican Former Migrant Workers in the United States. Federal and municipal bodies received them through the executive secretariat of the National Public Security System.
Panama	In August 2012, the National Assembly of Panama passed a bill amending the Fiscal Code and other reforms. This bill reintroduced the payment of estimated income tax in all declarations by legal entities instead of the monthly income tax advance (AMIR), which did not yield the financial results expected and proved unwieldy for the administration and taxpayers themselves. In June 2012 legislation was enacted to create the Panama Savings Fund (FAP), a long-term savings instrument to be funded with resources from additional income from the operation of the Panama Canal. Under the law, FAP will accumulate assets through contributions made by the Panama Canal Authorities to the treasury that exceed 3.5% of nominal GDP in the respective year, starting with fiscal year 2015. The law also specifies the conditions under which FAP may transfer funds to the treasury, including states of emergency, economic slowdown and prepayment of sovereign debt.
Peru	In June and July 2012, the Congress passed a law delegating the power to legislate on tax and customs matters and tax offences to the executive for a period of 45 days following its official publication. During this period the executive enacted a number of legislative decrees with a view to improving the country's competitiveness and increasing the tax take. Most of the measures will become operational on 1 January 2013.
Uruguay	The investment promotion regime was altered to optimize the evaluation indicators of investment projects (from January 2012) Top rates of domestic excise tax (IMESI) applicable to motor vehicles were changed (effective 1 October 2012) Elimination of VAT on sales to final consumers made using the Uruguay Social and BPS Prestaciones debit cards, which are used for withdrawing family benefit. In the last quarter of 2012, the government adopted a number of measures to promote tourism, including: exemption from VAT at hotels and restaurants and on car rentals, discount on fuel purchases at the border, a tax-free regime in Montevideo, Colonia and Punta del Este; and tax rebates for property rentals. IMESI was eliminated for certain personal care items.

Source: Economic Commission for Latin America and the Caribbean (ECLAC), on the basis of official information from the countries.

Public spending, and current spending in particular, increased sharply in a number of Latin American countries

Countries that had to cope with a sharp slowdown in their economies in the first half of the year showed more active fiscal policies, granting tax incentives and stepping up procurement and transfers (see table II.2). In Brazil, public-sector equipment procurement was increased with a view to stimulating investment, and a variety of tax cuts and exemptions were extended, particularly in the oil, industrial products and construction equipment sectors. In Argentina, capital transfers rose and social security benefits climbed sharply. In Paraguay, fiscal and economic performance was badly affected by the drought in the early part of the year.

Average public spending increased from 21.9% of GDP in 2011 to 22.9% in 2012, stimulating a degree of domestic demand growth in the face of slower or negative growth in external demand. This increase occurred essentially in current spending (0.6 percentage points of GDP), although average capital spending in the region also rose considerably, from 4.6 to 5.1 percentage points of GDP. Continuing their downward trend, interest payments represented just 1.7 percentage points of GDP in 2012.

Although spending rose across the board, the scale of the increase differed. The rise was quite sharp (over 1% of GD) in the Dominican Republic, Ecuador, Panama, Paraguay, the Plurinational State of Bolivia and Uruguay (over 1% of GDP) but more modest in other countries. The Bolivarian Republic of Venezuela, El Salvador, Guatemala and Honduras cut spending (as a share of GDP).

Capital spending was strongly up in the Dominican Republic and the Plurinational State of Bolivia, although current spending also rose. In Paraguay, estimates show current spending rising by more (4.3% of GDP) than capital spending (0.9%). In Uruguay, spending is estimated to have increased by 1.2% of GDP in 2012, owing to increased expenditure on social security and current transfers.

Figure II.5
LATIN AMERICA (19 COUNTRIES): CENTRAL GOVERNMENT
EXPENDITURE, 1990-2012
(Percentages of GDP)

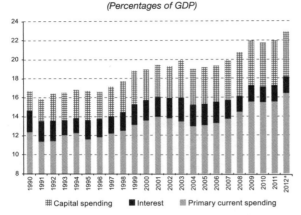

⊞ Capital spending   ■ Interest   ▨ Primary current spending

Source: Economic Commission for Latin America and the Caribbean (ECLAC), on the basis of official figures.
[a] Estimates.

In the Caribbean, starting from a much higher base, total revenue fell by 0.4 percentage points of GDP on average, although the drop was much greater in Antigua and Barbuda, Grenada, Jamaica and Trinidad and Tobago. Variations in spending were much more moderate, with the exception of substantial declines in Grenada, Jamaica and Saint Vincent and the Grenadines and large increases in Guyana and Trinidad and Tobago.

Efforts were made to tailor monetary policy to the weakness of aggregate external demand

With inflationary pressures moderate, monetary policy reference rates underwent some variations, while there was substantial growth in monetary aggregates. This reflected the authorities' efforts to cultivate the right monetary conditions to boost aggregate domestic demand. This stance was informed by a context of falling inflation and increasing concern about a further slowdown in aggregate external demand that was negatively affecting domestic economic activity.

Monetary policy rates were held steady in most of the region's countries during 2012. Changes were made, usually downward, in just eight of the 25 economies for which information is available (see table II.3).

Table II.3
LATIN AMERICA AND THE CARIBBEAN (SELECTED COUNTRIES): CHANGES IN MONETARY POLICY RATES, 2012 [a]

Unchanged	Upward	Downward	Changes of sign
Antigua and Barbuda	Chile (January, unchanged thereafter)	Brazil (cut seven times)	Argentina (cut in May and June, rising from July)
Bahamas		Dominican Republic (cut four times from June)	
Barbados			Colombia (rising until March, cut in August and September, unchanged thereafter)
Belize	Honduras (February and May, unchanged thereafter)	Guatemala (cut in July, unchanged thereafter)	
Bolivia (Plurinational State of)			
Costa Rica	Uruguay (up in January, then unchanged until October)	Paraguay (cut seven times)	
Dominica			
Grenada			
Haiti			
Jamaica			
Mexico			
Peru			
Saint Kitts and Nevis			
Saint Lucia			
Saint Vincent and the Grenadines			
Venezuela (Bolivarian Republic of)			

Source: Economic Commission for Latin America and the Caribbean (ECLAC), on the basis of official figures from the central banks of the countries concerned.
[a] Estimates.

Most countries with explicit inflation targets succeeded in keeping inflation within the limits set by the monetary authorities. A number of countries cut their monetary policy rates without imperilling their targets, examples being Brazil, the Dominican Republic, Guatemala and Paraguay, although inflation did pick up somewhat in the third quarter of the year, as will be seen in the following section. In these cases, as well as in Chile and Peru, where interest rates were left unchanged, lower inflation could be explained by the easing of external inflationary pressures in categories such as food (notwithstanding a short-lived international food price spike from June 2012) and energy, and in some cases by the effects of currency appreciation, which lowered the prices of imported goods and services.

Some countries experienced stronger inflationary pressures, but they differed in their policy approaches and outcomes. In Colombia, following a rise in the monetary policy rate in the early part of the year, the inflationary pressures of late 2011 eased and observed inflation dropped towards the middle of the target band. Despite upward movements in the monetary policy rate in Uruguay, inflation remained above the upper bound of the target band. In Mexico, the monetary authorities kept the policy rate unchanged despite a modest divergence between observed and targeted inflation.

Figure II.6
LATIN AMERICA (SELECTED COUNTRIES): OBSERVED AND TARGETED INFLATION,
JANUARY 2004 TO OCTOBER 2012
(Percentages)

A. Brazil

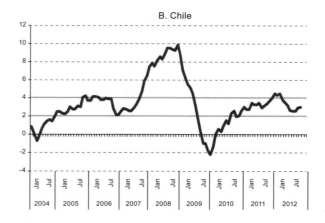

B. Chile

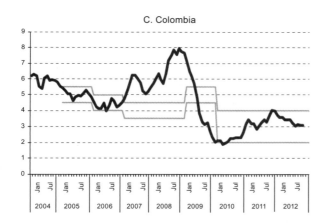

C. Colombia

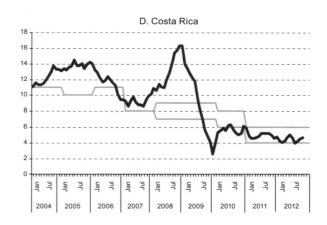

D. Costa Rica

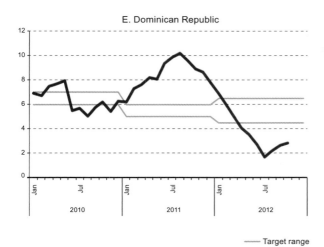

E. Dominican Republic

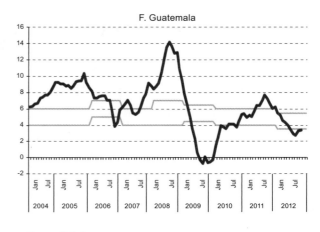

F. Guatemala

Target range   Observed inflation

Figure II.6 (concluded)

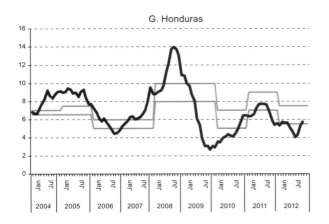

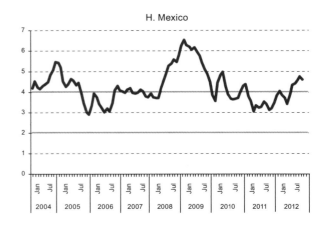

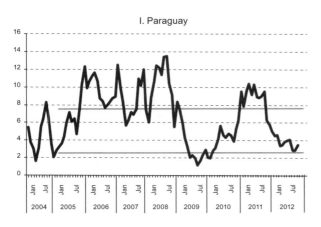

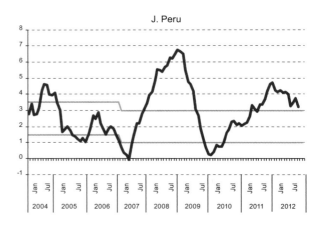

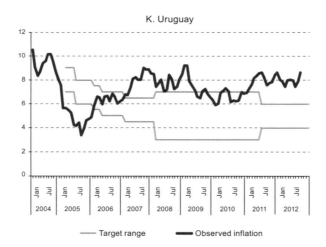

Source: Economic Commission for Latin America and the Caribbean (ECLAC), on the basis of official figures from the central banks of the countries concerned.

Meanwhile, liquidity injections by the monetary authorities, as measured by changes in the monetary base, continued to be substantial in 2012, with double-digit growth rates in 17 of the 25 countries for which information is available. Argentina, the Bolivarian Republic of Venezuela, Peru and Suriname stand out, with annualized growth in the monetary base exceeding 30% (see statistical annex).

Figure II.7
LATIN AMERICA AND THE CARIBBEAN (SELECTED COUNTRIES): CHANGE IN THE MONETARY BASE, SEPTEMBER 2011 TO SEPTEMBER 2012
(Percentages)

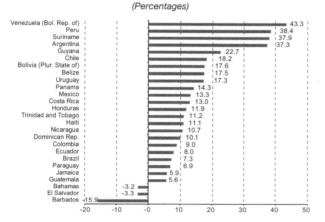

Source: Economic Commission for Latin America and the Caribbean (ECLAC), on the basis of official figures from the central banks of the countries concerned.

Similarly, the broader monetary aggregates (MI and M2) expanded in most of the region's countries albeit, as with the monetary base, mostly by less than in 2011. The cases of Argentina, Brazil, Nicaragua and Uruguay, where M2 growth slowed by over 10 percentage points, stand in contrast to that of the Bolivarian Republic of Venezuela, where M2 grew by almost 60%, nearly 20 percentage points over the 2011 rate. Another reflection of the authorities' intentions was the substantial increase in domestic lending during 2012, particularly to the private sector, with growth rates that exceeded 10% in 20 of the 31 countries for which information is available and approached or exceeded 30% in Argentina, the Bolivarian Republic of Venezuela, Guatemala, Haiti and Nicaragua (see figure II.8).

In Argentina, growth in lending to the private sector fell by 20 percentage points between 2011 and 2012, but in Barbados, the Bolivarian Republic of Venezuela, Guatemala and Jamaica it increased by over 13 percentage points. As regards the sectoral allocation of lending, consumer credit growth was particularly strong at 17%, followed by lending to commerce (13%) and industry (10%).

Figure II.8
LATIN AMERICA AND THE CARIBBEAN: CHANGE IN DOMESTIC LENDING TO THE PRIVATE SECTOR, SEPTEMBER 2011 TO SEPTEMBER 2012
(Percentages)

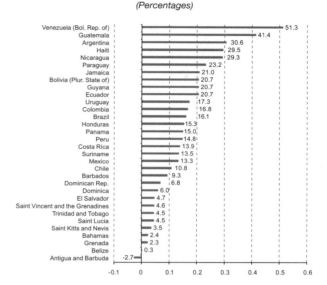

Source: Economic Commission for Latin America and the Caribbean (ECLAC), on the basis of official figures from central banks and other financial institutions in the countries concerned.

The combined effects of stable (and in some cases falling) policy rates, growth in the monetary base and the easing of inflationary pressures translated into a drop in interest rates, with lending rates falling in 17 of the 31 economies for which data are available and remaining unchanged in eight.

After picking up slightly in September, inflationary pressures eased

The inflation rate in the region fell for much of 2012. All subregions experienced an uptick in September and October, however, owing mainly to food prices pushed up by rising international prices as of July, and to supply constraints in some countries. Nevertheless, inflation rates remained below 2011 levels in most countries (see figure II.9). The region's weighted average inflation rate in the 12 months to October 2012 averaged 5.8%,[1] compared to a 6.9% cumulative 12-month rate for December 2011. By subregion, as in 2011, South America posted the highest rate of inflation, and Central America and the Caribbean saw the steepest drops. Argentina, Dominica, Jamaica, Mexico, Uruguay and Trinidad and Tobago were exceptions to the general trend of falling inflation in 2012, mainly reflecting higher food prices (see table II.4).

---

[1] As a simple average, the inflation rate was 4.5%.

Figure II.9
**LATIN AMERICA AND THE CARIBBEAN: 12-MONTH INFLATION,
JANUARY 2007 TO OCTOBER 2012**
(Percentages)

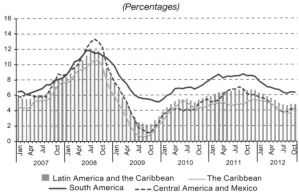

Source: Economic Commission for Latin America and the Caribbean (ECLAC), on the basis of official figures.

The region's highest inflation rates —into double digits— were recorded in Argentina and the Bolivarian Republic of Venezuela. The latter country also posted the largest drop in inflation, from 29% in 2011 to 18.5%[2] in 2012, as a result of increased availability of foreign exchange for food imports, lower international food prices early in the year and the implementation of legislation on costs and fair prices.[3] This law came into force in April 2012 and brought down prices mainly for food items, but also for personal hygiene items. Inflation fell significantly in Suriname[4] and Barbados, too, after being driven up in 2011 by rising prices for food, transport and fuels owing, in Suriname, to a 40% hike in fuel tax and, in Barbados, to higher prices for fuels and electricity, which fell in 2012.

Table II.4
**LATIN AMERICA AND THE CARIBBEAN: CONSUMER PRICE INDEX AND FOOD PRICE INDEX, 12-MONTH VARIATION,
SIMPLE AVERAGE, OCTOBER 2011 AND OCTOBER 2012**

	12-month inflation to October 2011		12-month inflation to October 2012	
	General CPI	CPI for food and beverages	General CPI	CPI for food and beverages
Latin America and the Caribbean	**6.4**	**7.5**	**4.6**	**6.2**
South America	**8.4**	**10.0**	**6.5**	**7.7**
Argentina	9.5	7.6	10.2	11.0
Bolivia (Plurinational State of)	6.9	8.0	4.3	4.3
Brazil	6.5	7.2	5.5	10.4
Chile	4.4	8.7	2.9	8.5
Colombia	3.8	5.3	3.1	3.6
Ecuador	5.4	7.1	4.9	7.0
Paraguay	4.9	5.1	3.4	-2.0
Peru	4.7	8.0	3.2	5.2
Uruguay	8.6	8.9	9.1	10.4
Venezuela (Bolivarian Republic of)	29.0	34.1	18.5	18.6
Central America and Mexico	**6.3**	**7.1**	**4.5**	**5.5**
Costa Rica	4.7	4.5	4.7	4.5
Dominican Republic	7.8	9.2	2.8	3.7
El Salvador	5.1	3.2	1.0	0.4
Guatemala	6.2	12.0	3.3	5.7
Haiti	8.3	9.0	6.5	7.2 [a]
Honduras	5.6	3.1	5.7	3.8
Mexico	3.8	6.0	4.6	9.8
Nicaragua	8.6	9.6	6.8	7.6
Panama	6.3	7.5	5.3	7.2
The Caribbean	**5.1**	**5.8**	**2.9**	**5.4**
Antigua and Barbuda	4.0	3.8	1.9	4.6 [a]
Bahamas	3.2	3.4	1.8	3.3 [b]
Barbados	9.6	9.8	2.8	4.6 [c]
Belize	1.9	...	0.5	... [a]
Dominica	1.3	2.9	1.7	4.0 [b]
Grenada	3.5	5.2	1.3	1.7 [b]
Guyana	3.3	2.5	...	...
Jamaica	6.0	5.4	6.7	11.4 [a]
Saint Kitts and Nevis	2.9	3.2	2.1	4.6 [a]
Saint Lucia	4.8	5.2	3.0	4.2 [b]
Saint Vincent and the Grenadines	4.7	4.9	1.9	2.1 [b]
Suriname	15.3	12.5	3.7	3.9 [a]
Trinidad and Tobago	5.3	10.4	7.7	14.7

Source: Economic Commission for Latin America and the Caribbean (ECLAC), on the basis of official figures.
[a] Data to September 2012, compared to September 2011.
[b] Data to August 2012, compared to August 2011.
[c] Data to July 2012, compared to July 2011.

---

[2] Refers to the 12-month rate of variation in October in the consumer price index of the metropolitan area of Caracas.
[3] This law is intended to cap prices for products considered to be basic necessities, in line with a cost assessment by the manufacturer and the behaviour of prices for imported raw materials.

[4] The rise in inflation in 2011 also reflected the local currency devaluation of 20% decreed early in the year.

Throughout 2012, core inflation in Latin America remained relatively stable as a regional average, and the largest impact on the regional consumer price index came from falling food price inflation. Food prices behaved differently in the Caribbean, however, reflecting the subregion's status as a net food importer and, in the case of Trinidad and Tobago, specific supply constraints (see figure II.10).

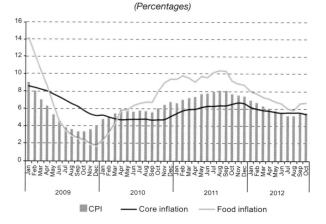

Figure II.10
LATIN AMERICA: INDICES FOR CONSUMER PRICES, FOOD PRICES AND CORE INFLATION, 12-MONTH VARIATION, SIMPLE AVERAGE, 2009-2012
(Percentages)

Source: Economic Commission for Latin America and the Caribbean (ECLAC), on the basis of official figures.

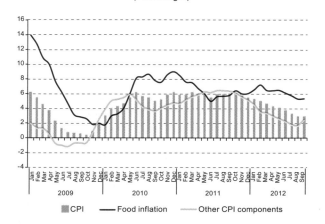

Figure II.11
THE CARIBBEAN: INDICES FOR CONSUMER PRICES, FOOD PRICES AND OTHER COMPONENTS OF THE CONSUMER PRICE INDEX, 12-MONTH VARIATION, SIMPLE AVERAGE, 2009-2012
(Percentages)

Source: Economic Commission for Latin America and the Caribbean (ECLAC), on the basis of official figures.

The pressure for currency appreciation eased but exchange-rate volatility increased in Brazil and Mexico

During 2012, a degree of deterioration in the current account owing to smaller capital inflows into the region, as reported in the relevant section of this edition of the *Preliminary Overview of the Economies of Latin America and the Caribbean*, affected the region's countries differently depending on the scale of the movements involved. Brazil carried on accumulating international reserves until May 2012, when the pressures eased, and the real subsequently depreciated, giving an average depreciation of 17.6% for the first nine months of the year. Mexico also accumulated reserves, while the peso exchange rate was volatile throughout the year, although on average it depreciated by 9.8% during the period. Where capital inflows remained high, however, as in Peru and Uruguay, the pressure for appreciation remained quite strong and these countries also accumulated reserves. The Peruvian sol appreciated by 4.1% and the Uruguayan peso by 2% on average during the first nine months of 2012, despite the authorities intervening in the currency market. Peru received substantial foreign direct investment (FDI) during the period.

As already noted, the deteriorating current account and smaller capital inflows into the region meant that the reserves build-up was slower than it had been in 2011, both as a share of GDP and in absolute terms. This was heavily influenced by the reduced build-up of reserves in Brazil from the first quarter of 2012, although the simple average of reserves in the region as a share of GDP rose from 15.6% to 15.8%, exceeding 25% of GDP in Peru and Uruguay and 50% of GDP in the Plurinational State of Bolivia (see figure II.12).

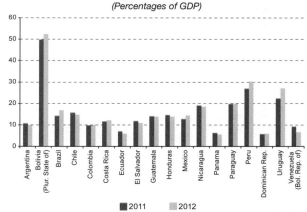

Figure II.12
LATIN AMERICA AND THE CARIBBEAN (SELECTED COUNTRIES): CHANGE IN INTERNATIONAL RESERVES, OCTOBER 2011 TO OCTOBER 2012
(Percentages of GDP)

Source: Economic Commission for Latin America and the Caribbean (ECLAC), on the basis of official figures.

A number of central banks intervened actively in the currency markets. Those of Argentina, Colombia, Costa Rica, Peru and Uruguay were particularly active (see table II.5). Meanwhile, although Brazil intervened in the currency market and built up reserves only until May 2012 (see figure II.13), the central bank intervened indirectly in August, September and October by using currency swaps to influence the path of the exchange rate.[5]

Table II.5
LATIN AMERICA (SELECTED COUNTRIES): CURRENCY MARKET INTERVENTIONS, JANUARY TO OCTOBER 2012
(Millions of dollars and percentages of GDP)

Country	Millions of dollars	Percentage of GDP
Perú	11 815	5.7
Argentina	8 073	1.8
Uruguay	725	1.5
Costa Rica	629	1.4
Colombia	3 959	1.1
Brazil	18 157	0.8

Source: Economic Commission for Latin America and the Caribbean (ECLAC), on the basis of official figures.

Figure II.13
LATIN AMERICA (SELECTED COUNTRIES): QUARTERLY EVOLUTION OF CURRENCY MARKET INTERVENTIONS
(Millions of dollars)

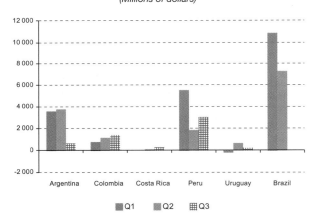

Source: Economic Commission for Latin America and the Caribbean (ECLAC), on the basis of official figures.

<hr>

[5] Swaps are a type of financial derivative whereby two parties undertake to swap currencies for a set period of time and at a certain price, with an undertaking to repurchase them at the end of the period. In October 2012, outstanding swap operations were worth US$ 4.9 billion.

In Brazil and Mexico, global financial instability exacerbated exchange-rate volatility. This was compounded by uncertainty about growth prospects in developed countries, especially the eurozone, by the volatility of international investors' risk appetite and by the strongly expansionary monetary policy conducted in the developed countries, especially by the United States Federal Reserve, but also by the European Central Bank and the Central Bank of Japan. Although the exchange rates of countries that are more deeply integrated into international financial markets had followed much the same path in 2011 amid the various shocks that year, the degree of correlation between their movements began to diminish in early 2012 (see figure II.14). The domestic currencies in Brazil and Mexico depreciated in nominal terms against the United States dollar, particularly as expectations about the future path of the European economy deteriorated during the third quarter of 2012.

Figure II.14
LATIN AMERICA (SELECTED COUNTRIES): NOMINAL EXCHANGE RATES AGAINST THE UNITED STATES DOLLAR, JANUARY 2008 TO NOVEMBER 2012
(Index: January 2008=100)

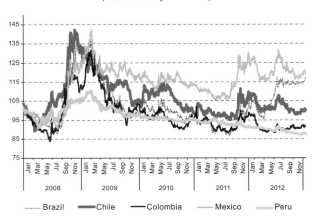

Source: Economic Commission for Latin America and the Caribbean (ECLAC), on the basis of official figures.

Nominal exchange-rate trends plus the dynamic of inflation in Latin America and the Caribbean led to the region's real effective extraregional exchange rate appreciating by an average of 2.7% during the first 10 months of 2012 as compared to the same period in 2011 (see figure II.15). The appreciation was greater in South America (4.8%, excluding Brazil) than in Central America (2.1%), being influenced particularly by the real effective appreciation in the Bolivarian Republic of Venezuela, owing to its high inflation and fixed exchange rate. The Caribbean subregion's real effective extraregional exchange rate rose by about as much as that of South America, with the main influence being the appreciation in Trinidad and Tobago. During the same period, conversely, Brazil and Mexico averaged real effective depreciations of 11.1% and 5.4%, respectively, against the currencies of countries outside the region.

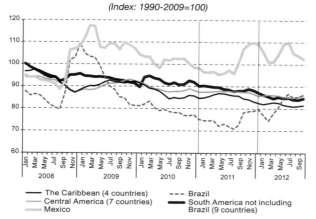

Figure II.15
LATIN AMERICA AND THE CARIBBEAN: REAL EFFECTIVE EXTRAREGIONAL EXCHANGE RATES, JANUARY 2008 TO SEPTEMBER 2012
(Index: 1990-2009=100)

— The Caribbean (4 countries)   --- Brazil
— Central America (7 countries)   — South America not including
— Mexico   Brazil (9 countries)

Source: Economic Commission for Latin America and the Caribbean (ECLAC), on the basis of official figures.

During the first nine months of 2012, the total real effective exchange rates of 15 countries in the region appreciated on average,[6] with effective depreciation in another six. To the instances of real effective currency appreciation already mentioned, namely the Bolivarian Republic of Venezuela (17.2%), Trinidad and Tobago (7.6%) and Peru (7.7%), may be added the Plurinational State of Bolivia (5.8%), where it resulted from the combination of a stable nominal exchange rate and the nominal depreciation of the Brazilian real, since Brazil is an important trading partner for the country. Mexico experienced a real effective depreciation of 5.4% and Brazil one of 11.7% in the same period, in contrast to the real-term appreciation seen in earlier episodes.

Countries continued their efforts to strengthen macroprudential policies

In 2012, a number of the region's countries implemented new macroprudential measures to strengthen their financial systems. The most common measures of this sort were changes to legal reserve requirements, currency market intervention as described earlier, and reforms to the regulatory frameworks of financial systems.

During 2012, Colombia, Honduras, Paraguay, Peru, the Plurinational State of Bolivia and Uruguay altered their legal reserve requirements, although not all for the same reasons. In Colombia, the authorities increased the reserve requirement to stem credit growth and thereby reduce the risks associated with overborrowing by households. In Paraguay, Peru, the Plurinational State of Bolivia and Uruguay, the authorities altered reserve requirements for foreign-currency deposits in an attempt to shift portfolio composition towards the local currency. In the Plurinational State of Bolivia, these measures brought foreign-currency deposits down by 7% in 2012, while in Peru the rate of growth in such deposits fell by over 12 percentage points. In Paraguay and Uruguay, foreign-currency deposits are still growing at rates of over 13%.

In Argentina, the Bahamas, Ecuador, Guatemala and Paraguay, regulators amended the rules governing the workings of their financial systems. In Guatemala, the aim of the reform was to reduce risk by setting limits on lending to shareholders of financial groups and to increase the amount of funding the central bank could provide to ailing banks. In Ecuador, the reforms dealt with countercyclical provisioning and increased the percentage contribution to the liquidity fund from 3% to 5%, while establishing a schedule of 1 percentage point increases to bring the contribution up to 10% for deposits subject to the legal reserve requirement. In the Bahamas, Ecuador and Paraguay, changes were made to the capitalization of financial institutions to reduce exposure to interest rate risks and other operating risks. In Argentina, a reform of the central bank's charter expanded its regulatory powers and amended the rules applying to foreign currency operations.

---

[6]   The total effective exchange rate is calculated from a country's trade with all its trading partners. The effective extraregional exchange rate excludes trade with partners in Latin America and the Caribbean.

Table II.6
LATIN AMERICA AND THE CARIBBEAN (SELECTED COUNTRIES): SUMMARY OF THE MAIN MONETARY POLICY, EXCHANGE-RATE
AND MACROPRUDENTIAL MEASURES ADOPTED, 2012

Country	Measures adopted
Argentina	• Reforms to financial regulations: (i) changes to the central bank charter, endowing it with greater powers of oversight and regulation and expanding its goals beyond the duty of ensuring the full employment of resources, (ii) new regulations on foreign currency transactions (both credit and debit transactions), and (iii) an increase in the minimum capital required to confront operating risks and interest rate risks and to open new branches and offices.
Bahamas	• Reforms to financial regulations: (i) new criteria were introduced for determining the capital and minimum capital required by financial institutions, especially those deemed to pose a systemic risk, and (ii) criteria and rules were laid down for reducing exposure to interest rate and solvency risks.
Bolivia (Plurinational State of)	• Reforms to financial regulations: the Legal Reserve Requirement Regulations were amended on two occasions with a view to encouraging and deepening financial remonetization. Provision was made for a gradual increase in the additional reserve requirement applicable to foreign currency deposits, leading to a total foreign currency reserve requirement of 65% in 2016. The second reform made an exception to the ban on early redemption for foreign currency time deposits converted into local currency, with a view to facilitating bolivianization. • Implementation of the foreign currency sales tax, payable by financial institutions when selling dollars at a rate of 0.7% of the total value of the transaction. The purpose of the measure is to further the bolivianization of the economy.
Brazil	• Currency market intervention to curb exchange-rate fluctuations. • A government campaign to bring down lending rates and spreads.
Colombia	• Currency market intervention to curb exchange-rate fluctuations. • Reforms to financial regulations: the central bank changed its regulations on the management of liquidity in the economy, stating what types of securities it could buy and sell, and how. • Changes in legal reserve requirement calculations to reduce liquidity growth in the money market and lower systemic exposure to credit risk.
Ecuador	• Reforms to financial regulations: the contribution of financial institutions to the liquidity fund was increased from 3% to 5%, with the additional stipulation that this contribution would increase by 1 percentage point a year up to 10% of deposits subject to the reserve requirement; the composition of minimum liquidity reserves and the percentage ratio of domestic liquidity were also reformed. • Reforms to financial regulations: rules were created for calculating countercyclical provisioning in each subsystem of the financial sector. • Reforms to the regulations on risk asset rating and provisioning, requiring institutions granting mortgages to set aside 100% of the difference between the cadastral and commercial valuations of the property being lent against.
Guatemala	• Reforms to financial regulations: the Congress passed a reform to the Banks and Financial Conglomerates Act whose purpose was to reduce risk in the financial system by setting limits on lending to shareholders in these groups and increase the amount of funding the central bank could provide to a troubled bank.
Guyana	• Currency market intervention to curb exchange-rate fluctuations.
Honduras	• Change in legal reserve requirement regulations: the procedure for depositing the legal reserve was changed so that, whether in local or foreign currency, this now had to be done in the form of demand deposits lodged with the central bank, with a minimum daily amount equivalent to 80% of the total.
Jamaica	• Currency market intervention to curb exchange-rate fluctuations.
Mexico	• Currency market intervention to curb exchange-rate fluctuations. .
Paraguay	• Reforms to financial regulations: measures were adopted to increase the capitalization of financial institutions so that they could confront the different types of risk associated with the financial market. • Change in the legal reserve requirement: changes were made to the legal reserve requirement rates applicable to foreign currency deposits and, to a lesser degree, local currency deposits as well, in order to reduce the exposure of the financial system to mismatches in the currencies in which its deposits and liabilities were denominated.
Peru	• Currency market intervention to curb exchange-rate fluctuations. • Change in the legal reserve requirement: the central bank increased the reserve requirement for both soles and foreign currencies on four occasions in 2012, raising it by 50 basis points the first three times and by 75 basis points the fourth, to control liquidity in the economy.
Trinidad and Tobago	• Currency market intervention to curb exchange-rate fluctuations.
Uruguay	• Change in the legal reserve requirement: the central bank raised the legal reserve requirement for both local and foreign currency deposits (although by more for the latter) to control liquidity in the economy.
Venezuela (Bolivarian Republic of)	• Reforms to financial regulations: the Government of the Bolivarian Republic of Venezuela amended its exchange-rate agreement to regulate the participation of Venezuelan private-sector organizations in the Transaction System for Foreign Currency Denominated Securities (SITME) and the instruments that would be available.

Source: Economic Commission for Latin America and the Caribbean (ECLAC), on the basis of official information from the central banks and finance ministries of the countries concerned.

Chapter III

Performance of the domestic economy: activity, employment and wages

Growth was slower in Latin America and the Caribbean in 2012, although several economies maintained their momentum

With the global economy faltering, the slowdown observed in the region's economies throughout 2011 continued in 2012, although the results varied from one country to the next. GDP in Latin America and the Caribbean rose by 3.1%, resulting in a 2.0% increase in regional per capita GDP. The region's performance is due mainly to lower growth in two of its major economies: Argentina (2.2% in 2012, down from 8.9% in 2011) and Brazil (1.2% compared with 2.7% in 2011) (see figure III.1).[1] Without these two countries, the rise in regional GDP would have been 4.3%, a figure similar to the previous year's excluding those two countries (4.5%).

Figure III.1
LATIN AMERICA AND THE CARIBBEAN (SELECTED COUNTRIES AND GROUPS OF COUNTRIES): CONTRIBUTION TO REGIONAL GDP GROWTH, 2000-2013
(Percentages based on dollars at constant 2005 prices)

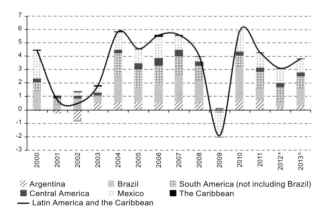

The Mexican economy expanded by 3.8%, while growth rates in the countries listed below were as follows: Costa Rica and Plurinational State of Bolivia (5%), Bolivarian Republic of Venezuela (5.3%), Chile (5.5%) and Peru (6.2%). At 10.5%, growth in Panama was the strongest in the region, while Paraguay recorded a 1.8% contraction. The remaining economies in Latin America and the Caribbean grew by between 1% and 5% (see figure III.2).

In terms of the performance by subregion, whereas South America recorded higher GDP growth than Central America in the period 2002-2011, the situation was reversed in 2012 with the former registering 2.7% and the latter 4.2%. The trend in the Caribbean subregion differs from that of Latin America, as it shows a modest improvement in 2012, with growth standing at 1.1%, up slightly over the 2010 and 2011 figures. With the exception of Jamaica and Saint Kitts and Nevis, the countries in the Caribbean achieved positive growth in 2012.

---

[1]   These two economies accounted for approximately 41.5% of regional GDP.

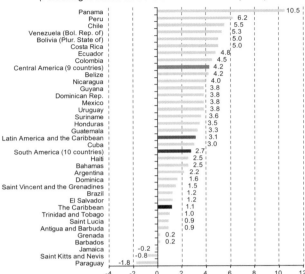

Figure III.2
LATIN AMERICA AND THE CARIBBEAN: GDP GROWTH RATES, 2012 [a]
(Percentages based on dollars at constant 2005 prices)

Source: Economic Commission for Latin America and the Caribbean (ECLAC), on the basis of official figures.
[a] Estimates.

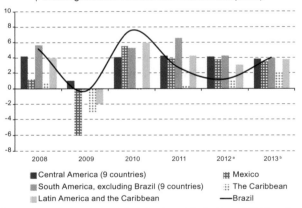

Figure III.3
LATIN AMERICA AND THE CARIBBEAN (SELECTED COUNTRIES AND GROUPS OF COUNTRIES): GDP GROWTH, 2012
(Percentages based on dollars at constant 2005 prices)

- Central America (9 countries)
- South America, excluding Brazil (9 countries)
- Latin America and the Caribbean
- ⊞ Mexico
- ⠶ The Caribbean
- —Brazil

Source: Economic Commission for Latin America and the Caribbean (ECLAC), on the basis of official figures.
[a] Estimates.
[b] Projections.

In aggregate regional terms, economic activity in the region reflected two opposing trends in 2012: the slowdown observed in 2011 continued into the first half of 2012, albeit not with the same intensity in all countries; in the third quarter, however, the regional economy started to pick up, thanks largely to the tenuous recovery in the Brazilian economy.

Consumption remained the leading component of growth

Regional growth was driven primarily by robust domestic demand, with both private and public consumption trending upward (by 3.7% and 3.9%, respectively). The increase in private consumption is reportedly based mainly on the expansion of credit to the private sector and on the continuous improvements in labour indicators. Higher remittances to Central America and the Caribbean also helped to boost this aggregate. The rise in public consumption contributed significantly to job creation in this sector.

Gross fixed capital formation rose by 4%, with mixed performances among countries (figure III.5). Argentina, Brazil and Paraguay recorded contractions, while the Bolivarian Republic of Venezuela, Chile, Ecuador, Peru, Plurinational State of Bolivia and Uruguay registered increases close to, or in excess of, 10%. Buoyant investment in the second group of countries appears to have been underpinned by the rise in the construction sector. Sustained growth in investment will have boosted the investment ratio, measured as gross fixed capital formation over GDP based on dollars at constant 2005 prices, to 22.9% (compared with 22.7% in 2011), the highest value recorded since 1981. Nevertheless, investment patterns varied appreciably from one country to the next: Argentina, Brazil and Paraguay saw reductions in gross fixed capital formation and, thus, a decline in their investment ratios (see figure III.5).

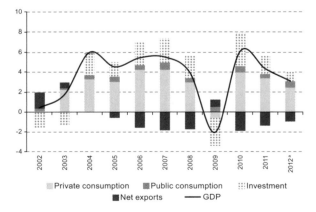

Figure III.4
LATIN AMERICA: GDP GROWTH AND CONTRIBUTION TO GROWTH BY THE COMPONENTS OF AGGREGATE DEMAND, 2002-2012
(Percentages based on dollars at constant 2005 prices)

- Private consumption
- Public consumption
- ⠶Investment
- Net exports
- — GDP

Source: Economic Commission for Latin America and the Caribbean (ECLAC), on the basis of official figures.
[a] Estimates.

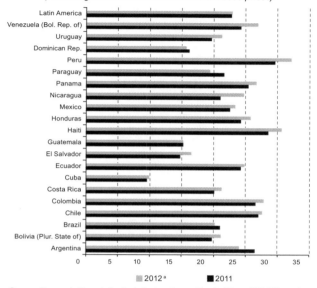

Figure III.5
LATIN AMERICA: GROSS FIXED CAPITAL FORMATION AS A PERCENTAGE OF GDP, 2011-2012
(Percentages based on dollars at constant 2005 prices)

■ 2012ᵃ ■ 2011

Source: Economic Commission for Latin America and the Caribbean (ECLAC), on the basis of official figures.
ᵃ Estimates.

At the regional level, loss of momentum in domestic demand meant that real imports of goods and services were less brisk at 4.7%, reflecting more moderate growth in consumption and investment across the region as a whole. Meanwhile, real exports of goods and services expanded by 3.7%. With real regional imports slowing even more sharply in comparison with 2011, net exports again contributed negatively to growth but less so than in 2011.

Commerce, construction and financial and business services were more buoyant

The performance of domestic demand was matched by a rise in domestic economic activity, especially in the services sectors (commerce, restaurants and hotels, and financial and business services) and in construction. Services activities expanded strongly across-the-board, with all countries recording positive growth. Commerce, restaurants and hotels benefited from the rally in tourism activity in 2012. Central America recorded the sharpest increase in international tourist arrivals (6.6% compared with 4.4% in 2011), while the expansion in South America (5.8%) was not as significant as in 2011 (9.4%). In the Caribbean, the performance was mixed: Barbados and some of the countries of the Eastern Caribbean Currency Union (ECCU) saw a decline in value added in the tourism sector, but elsewhere in the subregion, stronger tourist inflows contributed to a recovery in this sector and boosted economic activity.

The goods-producing sectors had mixed results. Agriculture contracted in Argentina, Brazil and Paraguay, following the severe drought that swept through these countries in early 2012. Trinidad and Tobago experienced a similar contraction due to adverse weather conditions, while the fall in agricultural output in Saint Lucia and Saint Vincent and the Grenadines was attributable to a disease affecting the banana crop. Mining performed modestly except in Colombia, Guatemala, Guyana and Panama. Industrial activity expanded in Costa Rica, Dominican Republic, Mexico and Nicaragua, but fell in Argentina, Brazil and Trinidad and Tobago. The construction sector recorded double-digit expansion in Bolivarian Republic of Venezuela, Ecuador, Panama, Peru and Uruguay, unlike the situation in Argentina and Paraguay, where it contracted.

Gross national disposable income expanded at a similar rate to GDP

With raw material prices falling in international markets, even though the prices of some exports (petroleum, gold, soybean and beef) actually increased, terms-of-trade gains diminished in relation to 2011. As a percentage of GDP, these gains, which had increased steadily between 2003 and 2008 and once again between 2009 and 2011, declined in 2012. Consequently, the region's gross national disposable income, measured in constant prices, showed growth below that of GDP (2.8%). South America was the subregion that recorded the sharpest slowdown in national income, followed by Central America, where higher migrants' remittances were not sufficient to offset the deterioration in the terms of trade. National income in Mexico continued to grow at much the same pace as GDP (see figure III.6).

Figure III.6
LATIN AMERICA: GROWTH OF GROSS NATIONAL DISPOSABLE INCOME, 2003-2012
(Percentages based on dollars at constant 2005 prices)

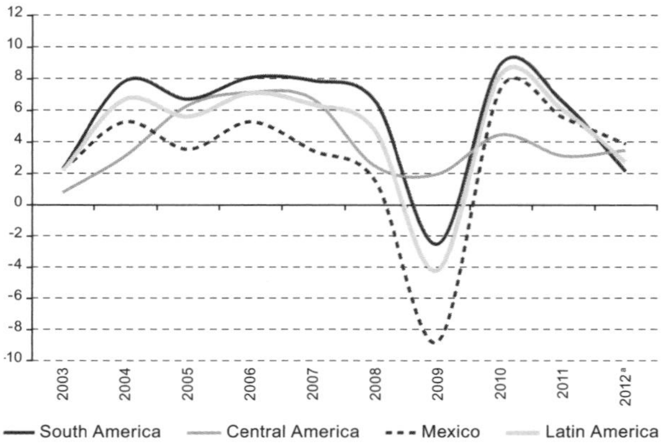

—— South America —— Central America - - - Mexico —— Latin America

Source: Economic Commission for Latin America and the Caribbean (ECLAC), on the basis of official figures.
ᵃ Estimates.

The trends described above can also be observed within countries. Figure III.7 compares the growth rates of gross national disposable income and GDP in Latin America for 2011 and 2012 (see figure III.7). In 2012, the rate of growth of national income slowed significantly and the

number of countries in which this growth rate is below that of GDP has increased substantially in relation to 2011. Lower growth in national income represents a change with respect to the trends prevailing between 2003-2008 and 2010-2011, and results in a smaller build-up of savings.

Figure III.7
LATIN AMERICA: VARIATION IN GROSS NATIONAL DISPOSABLE INCOME AND GDP, 2011 AND 2012
(Percentages based on dollars in constant 2005 prices)

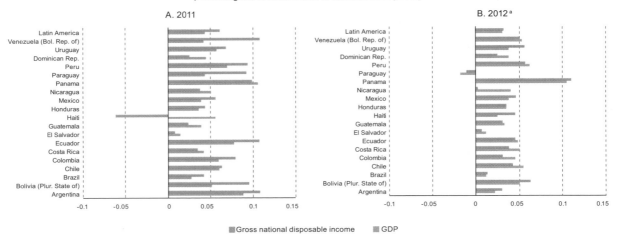

Source: Economic Commission for Latin America and the Caribbean (ECLAC), on the basis of official figures.
[a] Estimates.

External saving has played an increasing role in financing investment

Measured as a percentage of GDP based on current dollars, national saving grew by 0.5 percentage points in regional terms to stand at 21.4%, thus maintaining the upward trend observed since 2009, but remaining below those of the period 2006-2008. External saving expanded to 1.5% (up from 1.3% in 2011). As a result, gross capital investment in Latin America rose to 22.9%, slightly higher than in 2011 (22.2%), but below the 2008 figure (23.7%), the highest recorded since 1990 (see figure III.8).

Employment continued to rise but more slowly

With the slowdown in economic growth in Latin America and the Caribbean, the upturn in employment was moderate, especially when compared with the situation in 2010 in the immediate aftermath of the 2008-2009 economic and financial crisis. Having declined from 8.1% to 7.3% in 2010 and to 6.7% in 2011, the urban unemployment rate edged down more slightly to stand at 6.4% in 2012. The absolute number of urban unemployed in the region declined by 300,000 to stand at approximately 15 million persons. Bearing in mind that economic

activity was expanding more slowly, this reduction is in line with the pattern observed in the past 12 years, when each percentage-point increase in economic growth was associated with a 0.2-percentage-point reduction in the unemployment rate (see figure III.9).

Figure III.8
LATIN AMERICA: FINANCING OF GROSS DOMESTIC INVESTMENT, 1990-2012
(Percentages of GDP based on current dollars)

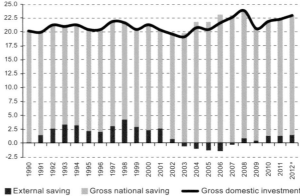

Source: Economic Commission for Latin America and the Caribbean (ECLAC), on the basis of official figures.
[a] Estimates.

Figure III.9

LATIN AMERICA AND THE CARIBBEAN: ECONOMIC GROWTH AND THE VARIATION IN UNEMPLOYMENT, 2000-2012

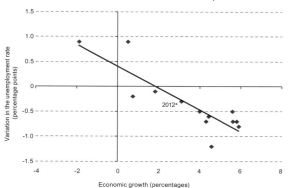

Source: Economic Commission for Latin America and the Caribbean (ECLAC), on the basis of official figures from the countries.
[a] Estimates.

The combination of an expansion in the economically active population in Latin America and the Caribbean with an even greater increase in employment, led to a 0.3 percentage-point decline in unemployment in 2012. The recent trend in Latin America and the Caribbean as a whole had been for a 0.1 percentage-point rise in the overall participation rate per year, but in 2012, the increase was 0.2 percentage points, owing to the higher number of job-seekers. Moreover, in the past few years, the employment rate had been increasing by 0.15 percentage points for each 1% increase in GDP. In 2012, when GDP grew by 3.1%, the employment rate rose by 0.4 percentage points, as observed in figure III.10, which is slightly higher than the historical trend. In short, the more substantial rise in the employment rate (0.4 percentage points) compared with the participation rate increase (0.2 percentage points) brought the unemployment rate down by approximately 0.3 percentage points.

Figure III.10

LATIN AMERICA AND THE CARIBBEAN: ECONOMIC GROWTH AND THE VARIATION IN THE URBAN EMPLOYMENT RATE, 2000-2012

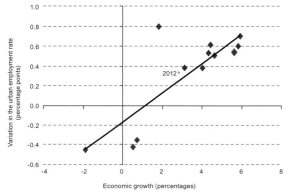

Source: Economic Commission for Latin America and the Caribbean (ECLAC), on the basis of official figures from the countries.
[a] Estimates.

Bearing in mind the level of economic growth, the fact that the employment rate is slightly above expectations suggests that the new jobs created in 2012 may have been concentrated primarily in labour-intensive activities, such as services and construction, including public-sector employment, as occurred in Brazil.[2] Employment rose and unemployment fell in the first three quarters of 2012 in Brazil, albeit more gradually than in previous years (see figure III.11). These indicators have still not returned to the pre-crisis levels in Mexico, the country in the region hardest hit by the 2008-2009 global economic crisis and where the labour market was seriously undermined. The employment rate trended upward quite vigorously in 2012, while the unemployment rate continued to slide gradually. Elsewhere in South America, similar to the situation in Brazil, employment and unemployment rates continued to improve over the year, albeit with a clear slowdown compared to previous years.

The situation in the Caribbean is more complex as the 2008-2009 crisis had a more lasting impact. The unemployment rate in this subregion started to rise significantly after the crisis and up to the first half of 2012 had not yet begun to fall, while the employment rate showed little variation. In Central America (for which no quarterly data are available), the trend has been similar to that of Mexico, with strong repercussions of the crisis in 2009 and some degree of recovery subsequently, but not sufficient to regain in 2012 the employment and unemployment levels recorded in 2008.

Based on the simple average of 15 countries for which sex-disaggregated, labour-market information is available, increases in employment levels during the first three quarters of the year related mainly to women: the female employment rate rose by 0.4 percentage points, while the male rate remained unchanged. The long-term upward trend in the female participation rate was maintained (0.3 percentage points), while the male participation rate diminished in many countries, which on average resulted in a 0.1 percentage-point reduction. Consequently, the female unemployment rate contracted more than the male rate (0.3 percentage points for the former, compared with 0.1 percentage points for the latter). Notwithstanding recent advances, disparities between men and women in terms of participation, employment and unemployment continue to be highly unfavourable towards women.[3]

---

[2] Rising employment in Brazil at a time when growth was slowing and was significantly lower than in the other countries of the region represents a shift from previous trends. While only partial information is available, since it relates only to the six metropolitan areas, one indicator that would account at least in part for this development is the breakdown of economic growth and new employment, with labour-intensive activities, such as services and construction, accounting for the bulk of new jobs. Moreover, public-sector employment increased more than proportionally in 2012.

[3] In 2011, the open urban unemployment rate, based on the simple average for 19 Latin American and Caribbean countries, was 6.6% for men and 8.8% for women.

Figure III.11
LATIN AMERICA AND THE CARIBBEAN (SELECTED COUNTRIES AND GROUPS OF COUNTRIES): URBAN EMPLOYMENT AND UNEMPLOYMENT RATES, 2008-2012
(Percentages)

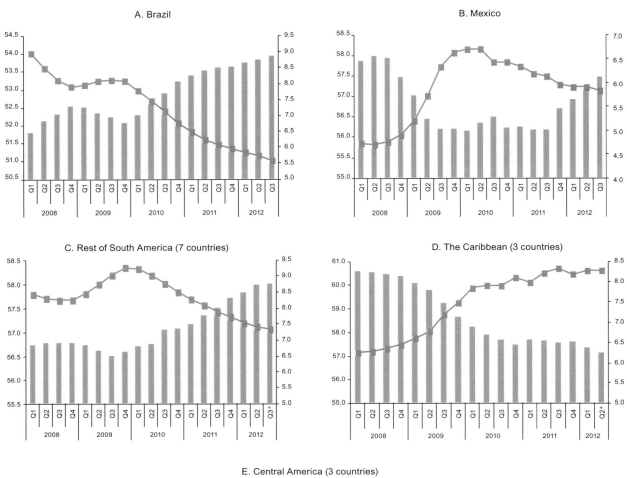

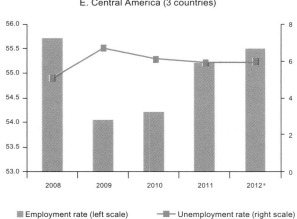

E. Central America (3 countries)

■ Employment rate (left scale)   ■— Unemployment rate (right scale)

Source: Economic Commission for Latin America and the Caribbean (ECLAC), on the basis of official figures from the countries.
[a] Estimates.

Employment quality improved slightly

Most new jobs created in the region were in wage employment. Following the economic slowdown and the cyclical behaviour of wage employment, however, this category of employment expanded at a slower pace than in previous years: 2.7% in the first three quarters of 2012, compared with 3.2% in 2011. By contrast, own-account work expanded more rapidly, growing by 2.2% in the first nine months of 2012, compared with the same period of 2011, slightly more than during that year (1.9%) (see figure III.12).

Figure III.12
**LATIN AMERICA AND THE CARIBBEAN: ECONOMIC GROWTH
AND JOB CREATION, 2000-2012**
(Percentages)

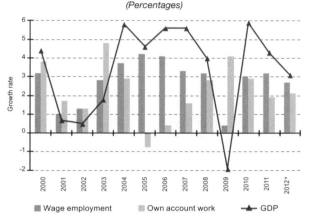

■ Wage employment   ■ Own account work   ▲ GDP

Source: Economic Commission for Latin America and the Caribbean (ECLAC), on the basis of official figures from the countries.
ª The figure for economic growth in 2012 is an estimate. The data relating to employment show the variation between the period January-September 2012 and the same period in the previous year.

Wage employment continued to grow more than own-account work in the Bolivarian Republic of Venezuela, Brazil, Chile, Colombia, Panama and Peru, but the opposite trend was observed in Argentina, Dominican Republic, Mexico and Paraguay, which, with exceptions, points to a connection between more (or less) robust growth and higher (or lower) generation of wage employment.

The pattern of growth in 2012 depended more on the increase in consumption, with a growing contribution by current public expenditure and relatively robust job creation in the public sector in several countries. In Argentina, Bolivarian Republic of Venezuela, Brazil, Chile, Dominican Republic and Paraguay, this type of employment grew faster than private-sector wage employment. By contrast, in Colombia, Mexico and Panama, private-sector wage employment expanded more substantially. In the median of nine countries public employment contributed almost a quarter to job creation in the first nine months of 2012, while private employment accounted for 40%. This

contrasts sharply with the situation in 2011, when private wage employment accounted for 64% of new jobs and the public sector for only 7%.

The review of the trends in formal employment reveals positive contributions but of lesser magnitude than in previous years. This applies in particular to Brazil, where a steady slowdown in formal job creation was observed in the first three quarters of 2012. This type of employment, which is usually of better quality, remained buoyant in Chile, Mexico, Nicaragua and Peru; the year-on-year rates in Peru were lower at the start of the year.[4] Average figures for the first nine months of the year indicate increases of over 3% in almost all countries for which information is available on trends in formal wage employment, which suggests that this category now accounts for a larger share of total employment.[5]

Figure III.13
**LATIN AMERICA (9 COUNTRIES): YEAR-ON-YEAR VARIATION
IN EMPLOYMENT, 2009-2012**
(Percentages)

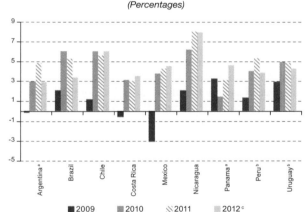

■ 2009   ■ 2010   ░ 2011   ■ 2012 ᶜ

Source: Economic Commission for Latin America and the Caribbean (ECLAC), on the basis of official figures released by the countries.
ª The data for 2012 relate only to the first half of the year.
ᵇ The data for 2012 relate to the period January-August.
ᶜ Year-on-year variation in the period January-September.

As is usually the case in the region in situations other than economic crises, the breakdown of employment by branch of activity shows a decline in the share of the agricultural sector. Employment in the manufacturing sector also fell in the first three quarters of the year in several countries, including the largest economies of the region (Argentina, Brazil and Mexico). Construction accounted for a larger share in countries such as Argentina, Brazil and Colombia but was lower in the Bolivarian

---

4   No information is available from administrative records in Colombia, but household survey data show an increase in the proportion of employed persons who contribute to social-security systems in this country.

5   Not all new formal jobs mean that new posts have been created, as they may also be the result of labour formalization strategies applied in different countries of the region.

Republic of Venezuela, Jamaica and Mexico. In most of the countries for which information was available (seven out of ten), the tertiary sector, which in itself accounts for the majority of jobs in the region, saw its share of employment expand further; this is probably due to the sluggishness of the tradable sectors, such as agriculture and industry, which were more seriously affected by the slump in external demand.

Rising real wages also helped to push up consumption

In general, average formal wages continued to trend upward with increments that were for the most part moderate. The simple average of formal wages in 11 countries increased by 2.5% in real terms during the first three quarters of 2012 compared with the same period of the previous year (the median being 2.9%). Nevertheless, as shown in figure III.14, major differences may be observed between countries and Bolivarian Republic of Venezuela and Uruguay recorded increases of over 4%, while Colombia, Mexico and Nicaragua had real increases of 1% or less.

In some countries, the policy designed to raise the minimum wage contributed to an increase in labour income. In the course of the year, the nominal value of the minimum wage increased in 16 of the 21 countries for which information was available. Between January and October of 2012, the simple average of the minimum wages in these 21 countries increased by 3.5% in real terms compared with the same period of the previous year, while the median increased by 2.7%. The countries with high real increases (5% or more) included the Bolivarian Republic of Venezuela, Brazil, Ecuador, Panama, Peru, Plurinational State of Bolivia and Uruguay.

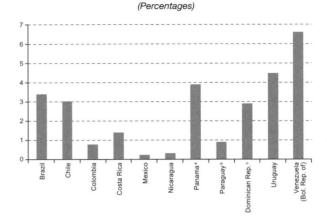

Figure III.14
LATIN AMERICA (11 COUNTRIES): YEAR-ON-YEAR VARIATION IN REAL AVERAGE WAGES IN THE FORMAL SECTOR, JANUARY-SEPTEMBER 2011 TO JANUARY-SEPTEMBER 2012
(Percentages)

Source: Economic Commission for Latin America and the Caribbean (ECLAC), on the basis of official figures from the countries.
[a] The data refer to the first half of the year.
[b] Refers to June.
[c] Refers to April.

The Bolivarian Republic of Venezuela and Mexico have introduced comprehensive reforms in their labour legislation. In the case of Mexico, the reforms include the introduction of new types of contract and the hourly payment system, the regulation of subcontracting and teleworking and the modification of some aspects of trades union organization. In the Bolivarian Republic of Venezuela, the working day was reduced, severance pay increased, outsourcing eliminated and postnatal leave extended. Other countries introduced reforms on specific aspects of labour regulation (see table III.1).

Table III.1
LATIN AMERICA (9 COUNTRIES): SOME OF THE LABOUR REFORMS INTRODUCED IN 2012

Bolivia (Plurinational State of)	Introduction of three days' paternity leave.
Brazil	Restructuring of social security contributions, which benefits labour-intensive activities.
Chile	Subsidy going to women and employers for hiring of women from vulnerable households.
Colombia	Regulation of teleworking.
Ecuador	Bringing working hours of domestic workers in line with those of other workers and regulation of their free time; extending the benefit of a shorter work day to all breastfeeding mothers for a period of 12 months.
Mexico	A series of reforms including: introduction of new types of contract (probation and apprenticeship) and an hourly pay system; regulation of subcontracting and teleworking; modification of the trades union organization; classification of employment of children under 14 years of age outside of the family circle as a crime; application of measures to improve security in the workplace, especially in mines; introduction of paternity leave; reduction of the working day during breastfeeding periods; prohibition of discriminatory action against women; restriction of the accumulation of overdue wages during labour litigation.
Nicaragua	Ratification of the Domestic Workers Convention, no 189, adopted in 2011 by the International Labour Organization (bringing the duration of the working day and the rights of domestic workers in line with those of other workers); new Labour and Social Security Code.
Uruguay	Ratification of the Domestic Workers Convention, no 189, adopted in 2011 by the International Labour Organization (bringing the duration of the working day and the rights of domestic workers in line with those of other workers); introduction of a partial unemployment subsidy regime.
Venezuela (Bolivarian Republic of)	A series of reforms including: reduction of the working week from 44 to 40 hours; increase in severance pay; extension of postnatal leave; introduction of 14 days of paternity leave; increase in period of security of tenure following birth of a child from one to two years (both parents); elimination of outsourcing.

Source: Economic Commission for Latin America and the Caribbean (ECLAC), on the basis of official figures.

Chapter IV

Outlook for 2013

The economic outlook for Latin America and the Caribbean depends to a large extent on how the world economy evolves in 2013. Significant progress was made in tackling the crisis in the eurozone countries in 2012, with agreements reached on the establishment of an institutional framework for promoting greater fiscal discipline and the formation of a single banking supervisor. The process of adopting and implementing these reforms in each country is complex and time-consuming. In the short term, the policy shift at the European Central Bank strengthened sovereign debt liquidity and succeeded in stabilizing this market, but problems of public debt sustainability persist. Moreover, borrowing requirements are expected to continue to rise in 2013, and will be exacerbated by the economic downturn. Although the adjustment processes have reduced the external disequilibria, in some cases the lack of competitiveness, an underlying, long-term problem and a key trigger of the crisis, remains to be resolved. Lastly, while some advances have been made, the challenge remains to restore financial system solvency and improve portfolio quality, which is a prerequisite for reviving the credit market. Recent studies suggest that this could start to occur in 2014.[1] In this context, the most likely scenario for 2013 is that Europe will continue to experience low growth with some countries even remaining in recession.

In the wake of the presidential elections in United States, prospects have improved for a fiscal agreement, albeit a partial one; meanwhile the Federal Reserve confirmed its intention to maintain an expansionary monetary policy for several years to come. Some positive performance indicators are now showing in labour and the real-estate market and, after four years of portfolio cleanup, the banking system is closer to resuming normal lending operations. These factors point to a more buoyant situation in 2013.

The situation in Europe also has an impact on exports from China and India, since the European market is a major outlet for these two countries' exports (17% and 19%, respectively). Domestic factors, such as the need to contain inflationary pressures in China and the limited fiscal space in India, will keep growth at much the same levels as in 2012 or slightly higher in the case of China.

[1]   Deutsche Bank, *Markets Research*, 2 December 2012.

The picture taking shape is thus one of slow overall growth and continuing uncertainty, which may worsen should geopolitical tensions disrupt the functioning of certain critical markets, such as the petroleum market.

In the light of this baseline scenario for 2013, regional GDP growth is projected at approximately 3.8%, partly thanks to higher growth in Argentina and Brazil. This will be due mainly to domestic factors, notably the recovery in the crop-farming sector in Argentina and in manufacturing and investment in Brazil; an upswing in trade between the two countries could also boost their respective economic activity levels. Domestic demand is projected to remain robust in several economies in the region thanks to the continuing improvements in labour indicators, an increase in bank lending to the private sector and raw material prices, whose high levels despite falls in 2012 bode well for the national income of commodity-exporting countries. Several countries have some scope for further countercyclical fiscal policies and for maintaining slightly expansionary monetary policies. External demand is unlikely to make much contribution to economic growth in 2013, given the persistence of a highly uncertain, low-growth external context. In terms of the subregions, growth rates will be less disparate with some acceleration expected in the Caribbean, although this may be countered by problems of fiscal sustainability, especially in countries whose main exports are services.

Underlying this gradual improvement in overall balances are efforts by the hardest hit economies to regain or defend their external competitiveness. The United States is seeking to recover its competitiveness as an exporter of manufactures (through production gains, but also through a strong expansion of its money supply, which tends to lower the value of the dollar). Clearly, other competitors in these markets are resisting this strategy. In Asia, China, Japan and the Republic of Korea are competing intensely for the competitive edge and this has led to major mutations in the distribution of production in some cutting-edge manufacturing sectors. In Europe, also, several countries are striving to retrieve their external competitiveness in manufacturing as well as in services (notably, tourism), as a necessary step along the path out of the current crisis.

These processes also affect Latin America and the Caribbean, not only in terms of their impact on the demand for the region's exports but also because its position in the distribution of world production will depend on the policies the countries adopt —on the production-development and institution-building fronts as well as in macroeconomic and trade matters— in response. Trade policies should help to tap regional demand by expanding intraregional trade. Macroeconomic policies should at the very least help to avert unsustainable real currency appreciations and support public finance sustainability by developing a tax burden robust enough to satisfy development needs (including public investment in economic and social infrastructure). By creating the conditions for a steady increase in private investment and applying policies geared towards raising productivity and reducing productive heterogeneity, progress can be made towards boosting growth over the long term.

Statistical annex

Table A-1
LATIN AMERICA AND THE CARIBBEAN: MAIN ECONOMIC INDICATORS

	2003	2004	2005	2006	2007	2008	2009	2010	2011	2012[a]
					Annual growth rates					
Gross domestic product [b]	1.8	5.8	4.6	5.6	5.6	4.0	-1.9	5.9	4.3	3.1
Per capita gross domestic product [b]	-1.0	4.5	3.3	4.3	4.4	2.8	-3.0	4.8	3.1	2.0
Consumer prices [c]	8.2	7.3	6.1	5.1	6.5	8.1	4.6	6.5	6.9	5.8
					Percentages					
Urban open unemployment	11.1	10.3	9.0	8.6	7.9	7.3	8.1	7.3	6.7	6.4
Total gross external debt/GDP [d][e]	39.9	34.5	25.1	21.1	19.7	17.4	20.2	20.0	19.4	19.7
Total gross external debt/ exports of goods and services [d][e]	169	138	101	84	83	74	101	96	89	90
					Millions of dollars					
Balance of payments [e]										
Current account balance	9 128	22 751	36 198	49 907	12 970	-33 082	-23 000	-55 482	-73 565	-88 606
Exports of goods f.o.b.	392 400	484 274	584 071	698 570	785 646	906 206	704 469	892 573	1 106 341	1 121 879
Imports of goods f.o.b.	353 771	430 019	510 156	608 037	723 734	868 022	653 463	846 401	1 035 729	1 073 892
Services trade balance	-9 052	-9 092	-8 881	-10 165	-16 485	-31 273	-31 439	-47 434	-65 020	-68 720
Income balance	-59 476	-68 747	-81 883	-94 929	-99 455	-107 772	-100 535	-116 033	-142 090	-130 281
Net current transfers	39 027	46 334	53 047	64 468	66 999	67 779	57 967	61 814	62 634	62 088
Capital and financial balance [f]	697	-7 181	24 856	13 453	112 617	71 575	69 217	141 750	179 399	141 393
Net foreign direct investment	39 790	50 212	57 309	32 519	92 803	99 425	70 740	74 795	125 851	114 778
Other capital movements	-39 093	-57 392	-32 453	-19 066	19 815	-27 850	-1 523	66 746	53 547	18 908
Overall balance	9 826	15 584	60 975	63 599	125 165	38 495	46 285	86 268	105 834	52 788
Variation in reserve assets [g]	-28 495	-24 438	-39 604	-50 932	-127 098	-42 123	-50 488	-87 747	-106 234	-52 824
Other financing	18 674	8 855	-21 371	-12 666	1 945	3 628	4 204	1 479	400	36
Net transfer of resources	-40 105	-67 073	-78 398	-94 143	15 107	-32 568	-27 114	27 195	37 709	11 149
International reserves	197 847	225 943	262 402	319 242	459 464	512 611	567 421	655 993	774 230	829 390
					Percentages of GDP					
Fiscal sector [h]										
Overall balance	-2.9	-1.8	-1.0	0.1	0.4	-0.2	-2.7	-1.7	-1.6	-2.0
Primary balance	-0.2	0.6	1.5	2.4	2.3	1.4	-0.9	-0.1	0.2	-0.3
Total revenue	17.0	17.2	18.2	19.4	20.2	20.5	19.3	20.0	20.4	20.9
Tax revenue	12.6	13.1	13.7	14.2	14.7	14.5	14.0	14.4	14.9	15.5
Total expenditure	19.9	18.9	19.1	19.3	19.8	20.7	21.9	21.7	21.9	22.9
Capital expenditure	3.7	3.6	3.6	3.6	4.0	4.5	4.5	4.6	4.6	5.1
Central-government public debt	57.0	51.2	43.2	36.1	30.7	29.7	31.0	30.4	30.5	29.9
Public debt of the non-financial public-sector	61.2	54.9	47.6	38.9	33.4	32.2	33.7	32.6	32.5	...

Source: Economic Commission for Latin America and the Caribbean (ECLAC), on the basis of official figures.
[a] Estimates.
[b] Based on official figures expressed in 2005 dollars.
[c] December-December variation.
[d] Estimates based on figures denominated in dollars at current prices.
[e] Does not include Cuba.
[f] Includes errors and omissions.
[g] A minus sign (-) indicates an increase in reserve assets.
[h] Central government, except for Panama and the Plurinational State of Bolivia, where coverage corresponds to the non-financial public sector, and Mexico, where coverage corresponds to the public sector. Simple averages for 19 countries.

Table A-2
LATIN AMERICA AND THE CARIBBEAN: GROSS DOMESTIC PRODUCT
(Annual growth rates)

	2003	2004	2005	2006	2007	2008	2009	2010	2011	2012[a]
Latin America and the Caribbean [b]	**1.8**	**5.8**	**4.6**	**5.6**	**5.6**	**4.0**	**-1.9**	**5.9**	**4.3**	**3.1**
Antigua and Barbuda	6.6	4.9	6.1	13.5	9.6	0.0	-11.9	-7.9	-5.0	0.9
Argentina	8.8	9.0	9.2	8.5	8.7	6.8	0.9	9.2	8.9	2.2
Bahamas	-1.3	0.9	3.4	2.5	1.4	-2.3	-4.9	0.2	1.6	2.5
Barbados	2.0	1.4	4.0	5.7	1.7	0.1	-3.7	0.2	0.4	0.2
Belize	9.3	4.6	3.0	4.7	1.3	3.6	0.0	2.7	2.3	4.2
Bolivia (Plurinational State of)	2.7	4.2	4.4	4.8	4.6	6.1	3.4	4.1	5.2	5.0
Brazil	1.1	5.7	3.2	4.0	6.1	5.2	-0.3	7.5	2.7	1.2
Chile	3.9	6.0	5.6	4.6	4.6	3.7	-1.0	6.1	6.0	5.5
Colombia	3.9	5.3	4.7	6.7	6.9	3.5	1.7	4.0	5.9	4.5
Costa Rica	6.4	4.3	5.9	8.8	7.9	2.7	-1.0	4.7	4.2	5.0
Cuba	3.8	5.8	11.2	12.1	7.3	4.1	1.4	2.4	2.7	3.0
Dominica	7.7	3.3	-0.5	4.4	6.0	7.7	-0.7	0.9	-0.3	1.6
Dominican Republic	-0.3	1.3	9.3	10.7	8.5	5.3	3.5	7.8	4.5	3.8
Ecuador	2.7	8.2	5.3	4.4	2.2	6.4	1.0	3.3	8.0	4.8
El Salvador	2.3	1.9	3.6	3.9	3.8	1.3	-3.1	1.4	1.5	1.2
Grenada	9.6	-1.0	13.5	-3.9	5.9	1.0	-6.6	0.0	1.0	0.2
Guatemala	2.5	3.2	3.3	5.4	6.3	3.3	0.5	2.9	3.9	3.3
Guyana	-0.6	1.6	-2.0	5.1	7.0	2.0	3.3	4.4	5.4	3.8
Haiti	0.4	-3.5	1.8	2.3	3.3	0.8	2.9	-5.4	5.6	2.5
Honduras	4.5	6.2	6.1	6.6	6.2	4.2	-2.1	2.8	3.6	3.5
Jamaica	3.7	1.3	0.9	2.9	1.4	-0.8	-3.5	-1.5	1.3	-0.2
Mexico	1.4	4.1	3.3	5.1	3.4	1.2	-6.0	5.6	3.9	3.8
Nicaragua	2.5	5.3	4.3	4.2	5.0	2.9	-1.4	3.1	5.1	4.0
Panama	4.2	7.5	7.2	8.5	12.1	10.1	3.9	7.5	10.8	10.5
Paraguay	4.3	4.1	2.1	4.8	5.4	6.4	-4.0	13.1	4.4	-1.8
Peru	4.0	5.0	6.8	7.7	8.9	9.8	0.9	8.8	6.9	6.2
Saint Kitts and Nevis	-1.4	4.4	9.9	4.7	2.8	4.7	-6.9	-2.4	2.1	-0.8
Saint Lucia	4.4	8.4	-1.9	9.3	1.5	5.3	0.1	0.4	1.3	0.9
Saint Vincent and the Grenadines	7.6	4.2	2.5	7.7	3.4	1.4	-2.2	-2.8	0.1	1.5
Suriname	6.8	0.5	4.5	4.7	4.6	4.1	3.5	4.5	4.5	3.6
Trinidad and Tobago	14.4	8.0	5.4	14.4	4.6	2.3	-3.0	0.0	-1.4	1.0
Uruguay	2.2	11.8	6.6	4.1	6.5	7.2	2.4	8.9	5.7	3.8
Venezuela (Bolivarian Republic of)	-7.8	18.3	10.3	9.9	8.8	5.3	-3.2	-1.5	4.2	5.3

Source: Economic Commission for Latin America and the Caribbean (ECLAC), on the basis of official figures.
[a] Estimates.
[b] Based on official figures expressed in 2005 dollars.
[c] Based in the new quarterly national accounts figures published by the country, base year 2005.

Table A-3
LATIN AMERICA AND THE CARIBBEAN: PER CAPITA GROSS DOMESTIC PRODUCT
(Annual growth rates)

	2003	2004	2005	2006	2007	2008	2009	2010	2011	2012[a]
Latin America and the Caribbean [b]	**-1.0**	**4.5**	**3.3**	**4.3**	**4.4**	**2.8**	**-3.0**	**4.8**	**3.1**	**2.0**
Antigua and Barbuda	1.3	3.5	4.8	12.2	8.4	-1.1	-12.8	-8.9	-6.0	-0.1
Argentina	5.8	8.1	8.2	7.5	7.7	5.8	0.0	8.2	7.9	1.3
Bahamas	-5.3	-0.6	1.9	1.0	0.0	-3.7	-6.2	-1.1	0.4	1.3
Barbados	1.3	1.2	3.8	5.5	1.5	-0.1	-3.9	0.0	0.2	0.0
Belize	1.9	2.3	0.8	2.4	-0.8	1.5	-2.0	0.7	0.3	2.2
Bolivia (Plurinational State of)	-3.2	2.2	2.6	3.0	2.8	4.4	1.7	2.5	3.5	3.5
Brazil	-2.9	4.4	2.0	2.9	5.1	4.2	-1.2	6.6	1.8	0.4
Chile	0.4	4.9	4.5	3.5	3.6	2.7	-2.0	5.1	5.0	4.6
Colombia [c]	-1.0	3.7	3.1	5.1	5.3	2.0	0.2	2.6	4.5	3.1
Costa Rica	0.2	2.4	4.1	7.0	6.2	1.2	-2.5	3.1	2.7	3.6
Cuba	2.8	5.5	11.0	12.0	7.2	4.1	1.5	2.4	2.7	3.0
Dominica	8.4	3.4	-0.2	4.8	6.4	8.1	-0.3	1.2	-0.2	1.6
Dominican Republic	-1.7	-0.2	7.7	9.1	7.0	3.8	2.1	6.3	3.1	2.5
Ecuador	1.0	6.4	3.6	2.8	0.6	4.8	-0.4	1.8	6.5	3.4
El Salvador	2.0	1.5	3.2	3.5	3.4	0.8	-3.6	0.8	0.9	0.6
Grenada	9.4	-1.3	13.2	-4.1	5.6	0.7	-6.9	-0.4	0.6	-0.2
Guatemala	0.0	0.6	0.7	2.8	3.7	0.8	-1.9	0.4	1.3	0.8
Guyana	-1.0	1.2	-2.3	4.8	6.8	1.8	3.1	4.2	5.2	3.6
Haiti	-1.2	-5.0	0.3	0.8	2.0	-0.5	1.5	-6.6	4.2	1.2
Honduras	2.5	4.1	4.0	4.5	4.1	2.2	-4.1	0.7	1.6	1.5
Jamaica	2.9	0.6	0.3	2.3	1.0	-1.2	-3.8	-1.9	0.9	-0.6
Mexico	0.2	2.8	2.0	3.7	2.1	-0.1	-7.2	4.3	2.7	2.6
Nicaragua	1.2	4.0	3.0	2.8	3.7	1.6	-2.7	1.8	3.6	2.5
Panama	2.3	5.6	5.3	6.7	10.2	8.3	2.2	5.8	9.2	8.8
Paraguay	2.3	2.1	0.2	2.9	3.5	4.5	-5.7	11.1	2.6	-3.4
Peru	2.7	3.7	5.6	6.6	7.7	8.6	-0.1	7.6	5.8	5.0
Saint Kitts and Nevis	-2.7	3.0	8.5	3.3	1.4	3.4	-8.1	-3.6	0.9	-2.0
Saint Lucia	3.4	7.4	-2.9	8.2	0.4	4.2	-0.9	-0.6	0.3	-0.1
Saint Vincent and the Grenadines	7.4	4.0	2.3	7.5	3.2	1.3	-2.3	-2.8	0.1	1.5
Suriname	5.4	-0.8	3.2	3.5	3.5	3.1	2.5	3.5	3.6	2.7
Trinidad and Tobago	14.0	7.6	5.0	14.0	4.2	1.9	-3.4	-0.4	-1.7	0.7
Uruguay	2.2	11.9	6.6	3.9	6.3	6.8	2.1	8.5	5.3	3.5
Venezuela (Bolivarian Republic of)	-9.4	16.2	8.4	8.0	6.9	3.5	-4.8	-3.1	2.6	3.7

Source: Economic Commission for Latin America and the Caribbean (ECLAC), on the basis of official figures.
[a] Estimates.
[b] Based on official figures expressed in 2005 dollars.
[c] Based in the new quarterly national accounts figures published by the country, base year 2005.

Table A-4
LATIN AMERICA AND THE CARIBBEAN: GROSS FIXED CAPITAL FORMATION [a]
(Percentages of GDP)

	2003	2004	2005	2006	2007	2008	2009	2010	2011	2012 [b]
Latin America and the Caribbean	**16.7**	**17.6**	**18.5**	**19.7**	**21.0**	**22.1**	**20.5**	**21.8**	**22.7**	**22.9**
Argentina	15.5	19.1	21.5	23.4	24.4	25.0	22.2	24.7	26.4	24.0
Bahamas	21.2	19.9	24.2	29.0	27.8	25.8	24.5	23.5	25.5	...
Belize	19.5	17.6	18.5	18.0	18.6	24.6	...	...	...	...
Bolivia (Plurinational State of)	13.4	12.7	13.0	13.5	14.6	16.3	16.2	16.8	19.7	21.2
Brazil	15.4	15.9	15.9	16.8	18.1	19.5	18.3	20.6	21.0	19.8
Chile	17.5	18.1	21.2	20.8	22.1	25.5	22.6	24.4	27.0	27.7
Colombia	17.2	18.2	19.7	21.8	23.3	24.7	24.0	24.1	26.6	27.9
Costa Rica	19.9	19.0	18.7	19.1	20.9	22.6	20.3	20.2	20.9	21.3
Cuba	8.2	8.3	9.0	11.5	11.0	11.4	10.1	9.6	...	...
Dominican Republic	16.3	15.8	16.4	17.9	18.6	19.3	15.9	17.3	16.2	15.6
Ecuador	20.0	19.4	20.4	20.5	20.8	22.7	22.3	22.8	24.3	24.9
El Salvador	16.6	15.5	15.3	16.5	17.1	16.0	13.3	13.5	14.8	16.5
Guatemala	18.9	18.1	18.3	20.1	19.8	18.1	15.6	14.9	15.2	15.3
Haiti	27.4	27.5	27.4	27.4	27.3	27.9	28.0	27.7	28.6	...
Honduras	23.1	26.8	24.9	26.5	31.0	31.6	21.1	22.0	24.2	25.1
Mexico	18.8	19.5	20.3	21.2	21.9	22.8	21.4	21.6	22.6	23.5
Nicaragua	21.5	21.8	23.0	22.5	23.7	23.3	19.3	19.0	21.0	24.6
Panama	16.7	16.9	16.8	18.1	22.7	25.9	23.4	24.3	25.4	26.4
Paraguay	16.4	16.5	16.6	16.5	17.6	19.5	18.9	20.3	21.6	19.4
Peru	17.0	17.5	18.3	20.2	22.9	27.5	25.0	29.0	29.6	32.2
Trinidad and Tobago	24.9	20.7	30.2	15.8	14.7	15.6	...	...	...	...
Uruguay	12.9	15.0	16.5	18.1	18.6	20.7	19.2	19.7	19.7	21.2
Venezuela (Bolivarian Republic of)	12.8	16.2	20.3	23.9	27.6	25.3	24.0	24.2	24.2	26.9

Source: Economic Commission for Latin America and the Caribbean (ECLAC), on the basis of official figures.
[a] Based on official figures expressed in 2005 dollars.
[b] Estimates.

Table A-5
LATIN AMERICA AND THE CARIBBEAN: BALANCE OF PAYMENTS
(Millions of dollars)

	Exports of goods f.o.b.			Exports of services			Imports of goods f.o.b.			Imports of services		
	2010	2011	2012[a]	2010	2011	2012[a]	2010	2011	2012[a]	2010	2011	2012[a]
Latin America and the Caribbean	**892 573**	**1 106 341**	**1 121 879**	**117 906**	**132 094**	**133 786**	**846 401**	**1 035 729**	**1 073 892**	**165 340**	**197 114**	**202 506**
Antigua and Barbuda	45	53	45	479	499	514	454	440	447	226	224	230
Argentina	68 134	83 950	81 903	13 556	15 481	15 688	53 868	70 743	65 774	14 703	17 721	19 545
Bahamas	702	834	889	2 494	2 606	2 762	2 590	2 965	3 439	1 181	1 292	1 319
Barbados	422	448	...	1 464	1 405	...	1 562	1 703	...	588	578	...
Belize	476	604	637	360	330	335	650	778	824	160	120	139
Bolivia (Plurinational State of)	6 390	8 332	9 682	769	801	803	5 380	7 664	8 259	1 032	1 123	1 136
Brazil	201 916	256 040	244 549	31 599	38 210	39 824	181 768	226 234	226 385	62 434	76 161	78 686
Chile	70 897	81 411	80 352	10 831	12 406	12 510	55 572	70 618	73 686	12 637	14 823	14 398
Colombia	40 867	57 739	61 415	4 446	4 856	5 209	38 628	52 230	55 927	8 070	9 503	10 642
Costa Rica	9 516	10 383	11 020	4 320	4 990	5 663	12 956	15 534	16 494	1 783	1 780	1 877
Dominica	36	34	...	147	148	157	198	204	...	67	69	...
Dominican Republic	6 754	8 536	9 016	5 154	5 341	5 733	15 489	17 423	17 811	2 185	2 232	2 277
Ecuador	18 137	23 082	24 923	1 472	1 587	1 783	19 641	23 243	24 904	3 011	3 166	3 394
El Salvador	4 577	5 401	5 340	976	1 073	1 214	8 107	9 647	9 890	1 070	1 106	1 147
Grenada	30	33	...	137	150	158	284	285	...	94	96	102
Guatemala	8 536	10 517	10 627	2 292	2 359	2 455	12 807	15 482	16 174	2 381	2 504	2 635
Guyana	885	1 129	1 232	248	298	...	1 419	1 771	1 939	344	434	...
Haiti	563	768	786	239	249	304	2 810	3 014	2 791	1 277	1 140	1 297
Honduras	6 111	7 800	7 474	976	1 023	1 149	8 907	10 994	10 882	1 169	1 461	1 597
Jamaica	1 370	1 663	1 732	2 634	2 649	...	4 629	5 923	5 600	1 824	1 951	...
Mexico	298 860	349 946	370 004	15 167	15 298	15 929	301 744	351 116	370 327	25 318	29 527	29 469
Nicaragua	3 158	4 057	4 270	573	660	711	4 792	6 125	6 563	719	838	907
Panama	12 680	16 929	18 025	6 070	7 150	7 671	17 235	22 946	24 321	2 648	3 336	3 823
Paraguay	8 520	10 389	9 287	1 473	1 917	1 840	9 916	12 066	11 123	755	903	848
Peru	35 565	46 268	45 384	3 693	4 364	5 089	28 815	36 967	40 220	6 038	6 497	7 238
Saint Kitts and Nevis	79	88	57	130	142	182	236	238	228	99	102	100
Saint Lucia	239	240	209	390	374	406	575	581	638	203	203	228
Saint Vincent and the Grenadines	45	42	...	139	145	149	298	307	...	91	94	96
Suriname	2 084	2 467	2 096	241	201	149	1 398	1 679	1 368	259	563	403
Trinidad and Tobago	11 204	15 067	14 235	876	...	...	6 504	9 304	10 048	391	...	...
Uruguay	8 031	9 281	10 227	2 706	3 528	3 439	8 558	10 691	11 437	1 535	2 014	2 230
Venezuela (Bolivarian Republic of)	65 745	92 811	96 461	1 857	1 855	1 961	38 613	46 813	56 393	11 048	15 552	16 814

Table A-5 (continued)

	Goods and services balance			Income balance			Current transfers balance			Current account balance		
	2010	2011	2012[a]	2010	2011	2012[a]	2010	2011	2012[a]	2010	2011	2012[a]
Latin America and the Caribbean	**-1 261**	**5 893**	**-20 413**	**-116 033**	**-142 090**	**-130 281**	**61 814**	**62 634**	**62 088**	**-55 482**	**-73 565**	**-88 606**
Antigua and Barbuda	-156	-112	-118	-32	-32	-34	22	22	23	-166	-122	-129
Argentina	13 119	10 967	12 272	-9 939	-10 737	-10 340	-388	-536	-446	2 791	-307	1 487
Bahamas	-575	-818	-1 107	-234	-236	-247	-3	-36	43	-811	-1 090	-1 310
Barbados	-264	-427	...	-121	-102	...	20	23	...	-366	-506	...
Belize	26	36	9	-158	-120	-108	92	43	74	-41	-42	-25
Bolivia (Plurinational State of)	747	346	1 089	-860	-986	-1 102	1 081	1 177	1 193	969	537	1 180
Brazil	-10 687	-8 145	-20 698	-39 486	-47 319	-36 383	2 902	2 985	2 994	-47 272	-52 481	-54 087
Chile	13 519	8 376	4 779	-14 765	-14 015	-12 379	4 515	2 418	1 536	3 269	-3 220	-6 064
Colombia	-1 384	862	55	-11 849	-15 831	-17 049	4 475	4 938	5 157	-8 758	-10 032	-11 836
Costa Rica	-902	-1 941	-1 688	-745	-567	-1 018	366	323	323	-1 281	-2 185	-2 383
Dominica	-82	-92	-77	-9	-8	-11	20	20	20	-71	-80	-68
Dominican Republic	-5 767	-5 778	-5 338	-1 686	-2 128	-2 371	3 124	3 406	3 292	-4 330	-4 499	-4 417
Ecuador	-3 042	-1 739	-1 593	-1 041	-1 223	-1 380	2 458	2 723	2 546	-1 625	-238	-427
El Salvador	-3 624	-4 279	-4 483	-551	-632	-749	3 599	3 841	4 082	-576	-1 070	-1 150
Grenada	-211	-198	-208	-51	-48	-44	32	31	27	-230	-215	-225
Guatemala	-4 361	-5 110	-5 728	-1 211	-1 553	-1 660	4 946	5 207	5 607	-626	-1 456	-1 781
Guyana	-630	-778	-909	13	-9	-10	371	415	469	-246	-373	-450
Haiti	-3 285	-3 137	-2 998	22	41	64	3 097	2 757	2 624	-166	-339	-310
Honduras	-2 989	-3 632	-3 855	-728	-974	-988	2 882	3 108	3 220	-836	-1 498	-1 623
Jamaica	-2 449	-3 563	-2 967	-495	-548	-313	2 010	2 043	2 007	-934	-2 069	-1 273
Mexico	-13 035	-15 400	-13 864	-10 171	-16 726	-16 499	21 537	22 974	22 502	-1 669	-9 153	-7 860
Nicaragua	-1 781	-2 246	-2 489	-275	-247	-286	1 173	1 192	1 311	-883	-1 302	-1 465
Panama	-1 133	-2 203	-2 448	-1 859	-1 799	-1 901	129	129	90	-2 862	-3 874	-4 260
Paraguay	-678	-664	-843	-533	-307	-317	557	701	692	-654	-270	-469
Peru	4 404	7 169	3 014	-11 212	-13 710	-12 450	3 026	3 200	3 302	-3 782	-3 341	-6 133
Saint Kitts and Nevis	-126	-111	-89	-34	-31	-27	46	46	53	-115	-96	-63
Saint Lucia	-149	-170	-251	-41	-40	-44	15	20	19	-175	-190	-275
Saint Vincent and the Grenadines	-206	-214	-204	-17	-16	-18	10	10	10	-213	-220	-212
Suriname	669	426	475	-102	-262	-152	87	87	71	653	251	394
Trinidad and Tobago	5 185	6 064	4 632	-1 058	-3 475	-2 591	65	33	28	4 192	2 623	2 070
Uruguay	644	104	-1	-1 501	-1 554	-1 517	118	126	119	-739	-1 324	-1 399
Venezuela (Bolivarian Republic of)	17 941	32 301	25 215	-5 302	-6 896	-8 357	-568	-790	-900	12 071	24 615	15 958

Table A-5 (concluded)

	Capital and financial balance [b]			Overall balance			Reserve assets (variation) [c]			Other financing		
	2010	2011	2012[a]	2010	2011	2012[a]	2010	2011	2012[a]	2010	2011	2012[a]
Latin America and the Caribbean	**141 750**	**179 399**	**141 393**	**86 268**	**105 834**	**52 788**	**-87 747**	**-106 234**	**-52 824**	**1 479**	**400**	**36**
Antigua and Barbuda	179	115	160	12	-7	31	-31	7	-31	19	0	...
Argentina	1 367	-5 801	-2 721	4 157	-6 108	-1 234	-4 157	6 108	1 234	0	0	...
Bahamas	856	1 114	1 145	45	24	-166	-45	-24	166	0	0	...
Barbados	400	473	...	34	-32	...	-34	32	...	0	0	...
Belize	45	60	51	4	18	26	-4	-18	-26	0	0	...
Bolivia (Plurinational State of)	-46	1 623	434	923	2 160	1 614	-923	-2 160	-1 614	0	0	...
Brazil	96 373	111 118	76 451	49 101	58 637	22 364	-49 101	-58 637	-22 364	0	0	...
Chile	-245	17 410	3 387	3 023	14 190	-2 677	-3 023	-14 190	2 677	0	0	...
Colombia	11 893	13 776	15 793	3 136	3 744	3 957	-3 136	-3 744	-3 957	0	0	...
Costa Rica	1 842	2 318	2 793	561	132	410	-561	-132	-410	0	0	...
Dominica	73	76	78	1	-4	10	-1	4	-10	0	0	...
Dominican Republic	4 387	4 653	2 774	58	154	-1 643	-453	-331	1 643	395	177	...
Ecuador	413	510	1 905	-1 212	272	1 479	1 170	-336	-1 479	42	64	...
El Salvador	281	656	1 684	-295	-414	534	295	414	-534	0	0	...
Grenada	221	205	225	-10	-9	...	10	9	...	0	0	...
Guatemala	1 303	1 661	2 432	677	206	651	-677	-206	-651	0	0	...
Guyana	363	358	469	117	-15	19	-155	-25	-19	38	40	...
Haiti	909	525	434	743	186	124	-845	-209	-156	102	23	32
Honduras	1 404	1 562	1 668	569	64	44	-592	-81	-49	24	17	4
Jamaica	586	1 864	1 900	-348	-205	627	-431	205	-627	779	0	...
Mexico	22 284	37 333	24 184	20 615	28 180	16 323	-20 615	-28 180	-16 323	0	0	...
Nicaragua	1 055	1 329	1 444	172	27	-20	-222	-73	20	50	46	...
Panama	3 313	3 527	3 908	452	-347	-352	-452	347	352	0	0	...
Paraguay	973	1 054	510	319	784	41	-319	-784	-41	0	0	...
Peru	14 955	8 032	18 371	11 173	4 691	12 238	-11 192	-4 724	-12 238	19	33	...
Saint Kitts and Nevis	147	142	90	33	45	27	-33	-45	-27	0	0	...
Saint Lucia	206	219	278	32	29	3	-32	-29	-3	0	0	...
Saint Vincent and the Grenadines	238	192	215	25	-28	3	-36	28	-3	10	0	...
Suriname	-619	-77	-231	34	174	163	-34	-174	-163	0	0	...
Trinidad and Tobago	-3 774	-1 870	-2 170	418	753	-100	-418	-753	100	0	0	...
Uruguay	378	3 888	3 973	-361	2 564	2 574	361	-2 564	-2 574	0	0	...
Venezuela (Bolivarian Republic of)	-20 010	-28 647	-20 241	-7 939	-4 032	-4 283	7 939	4 032	4 283	0	0	...

Source: Economic Commission for Latin America and the Caribbean (ECLAC), on the basis of official figures.
[a] Estimates.
[b] Includes errors and omissions.
[c] A minus sign (-) indicates an increase in reserve assets.

Table A-6
LATIN AMERICA AND THE CARIBBEAN: INTERNATIONAL TRADE OF GOODS
(Indices 2005=100)

EXPORTS OF GOODS, f.o.b.

	Value			Volume			Unit value		
	2010	2011	2012[a]	2010	2011	2012[a]	2010	2011	2012[a]
Latin America	**154.2**	**191.0**	**194.1**	**112.7**	**117.7**	**120.7**	**136.8**	**162.2**	**160.8**
Argentina	168.7	207.9	202.8	127.2	132.8	129.6	132.6	156.5	156.5
Bolivia (Plurinational State of)	226.1	294.8	342.5	124.2	133.8	150.0	182.0	220.3	228.4
Brazil	170.7	216.4	206.7	104.1	107.3	106.8	164.0	201.7	193.6
Chile	168.9	194.0	191.4	103.7	107.9	115.3	162.9	179.7	166.0
Colombia	188.1	265.7	282.6	128.1	147.1	153.4	146.8	180.6	184.2
Costa Rica	134.0	146.3	155.2	141.2	149.6	159.6	94.9	97.7	97.3
Dominican Republic	109.9	138.9	146.7	94.1	110.1	117.5	116.8	126.1	124.9
Ecuador	173.3	220.5	238.1	117.5	123.6	130.6	147.5	178.4	182.3
El Salvador	132.1	155.9	154.1	118.8	128.6	128.2	111.2	121.2	120.2
Guatemala	156.3	192.6	194.6	121.8	134.0	140.5	128.3	143.7	138.6
Haiti	122.6	167.1	171.1	103.2	137.8	135.8	118.8	121.3	125.9
Honduras	121.1	154.5	148.1	97.7	100.5	103.5	123.9	153.7	143.1
Mexico	139.2	163.0	172.4	121.0	123.2	127.9	115.1	132.3	134.8
Nicaragua	190.9	245.3	258.1	154.8	176.0	185.8	123.3	139.4	139.0
Panama	171.9	229.5	244.4	152.9	190.8	201.1	112.4	120.3	121.5
Paraguay	254.2	309.9	277.1	207.8	226.2	196.8	122.3	137.0	140.8
Peru	204.8	266.4	261.3	109.4	114.7	116.5	187.2	232.2	224.3
Uruguay	212.8	245.9	271.0	148.1	148.8	159.3	143.7	165.2	170.2
Venezuela (Bolivarian Republic of)	118.0	166.6	173.1	73.1	78.8	80.3	161.4	211.5	215.7

IMPORTS OF GOODS, f.o.b.

	Value			Volume			Unit value		
	2010	2011	2012[a]	2010	2011	2012[a]	2010	2011	2012[a]
Latin America	**170.3**	**208.2**	**216.4**	**141.1**	**156.9**	**161.0**	**120.6**	**132.7**	**134.4**
Argentina	197.3	259.1	240.9	176.2	209.2	187.7	112.0	123.9	128.3
Bolivia (Plurinational State of)	221.3	315.3	339.8	171.3	223.9	241.1	129.2	140.8	140.9
Brazil	246.9	307.4	307.6	189.9	207.4	206.5	130.0	148.2	149.0
Chile	181.2	230.3	240.3	162.4	188.3	188.9	111.6	122.3	127.2
Colombia	191.9	259.4	277.8	158.2	194.4	205.2	121.3	133.4	135.3
Costa Rica	139.9	167.8	178.1	135.4	151.7	161.1	103.4	110.6	110.6
Dominican Republic	156.9	176.5	180.5	136.8	135.0	138.0	114.7	130.8	130.8
Ecuador	202.3	239.4	256.5	161.9	174.1	185.1	125.0	137.5	138.6
El Salvador	124.7	148.4	152.1	105.8	115.5	117.9	117.8	128.4	129.0
Guatemala	132.7	160.4	167.6	104.8	112.1	116.2	126.7	143.1	144.2
Haiti	214.8	230.3	213.3	152.0	132.6	124.5	141.2	173.7	171.4
Honduras	136.1	168.0	166.3	106.0	114.4	112.4	128.4	146.8	148.0
Mexico	135.7	157.9	166.6	115.2	124.9	130.1	117.8	126.4	128.0
Nicaragua	162.1	207.2	222.0	134.4	151.3	161.8	120.7	136.9	137.3
Panama	192.9	256.9	272.3	162.0	197.2	206.6	119.1	130.3	131.8
Paraguay	260.0	316.3	291.6	229.0	254.7	235.1	113.5	124.2	124.1
Peru	238.5	306.0	332.9	162.6	189.7	203.5	146.6	161.3	163.6
Uruguay	228.0	284.8	304.7	174.9	193.4	205.6	130.4	147.3	148.2
Venezuela (Bolivarian Republic of)	160.8	195.0	234.9	139.3	154.9	184.8	115.5	125.8	127.1

Source: Economic Commission for Latin America and the Caribbean (ECLAC), on the basis of official figures.
[a] Estimates.

Table A-7
LATIN AMERICA: TERMS OF TRADE FOR GOODS f.o.b. / f.o.b.
(Indices 2005=100)

	2003	2004	2005	2006	2007	2008	2009	2010	2011	2012 [a]
Latin America	**91.0**	**95.3**	**100.0**	**106.8**	**109.6**	**113.0**	**103.3**	**113.4**	**122.3**	**119.6**
Argentina	100.3	102.2	100.0	106.0	110.0	124.6	118.9	118.4	126.3	121.9
Bolivia (Plurinational State of)	88.1	93.0	100.0	125.0	127.0	128.7	124.6	140.9	156.4	162.1
Brazil	97.8	98.7	100.0	105.3	107.5	111.3	108.7	126.1	136.1	130.0
Chile	73.5	89.3	100.0	131.1	135.6	117.9	119.3	146.0	146.9	130.5
Colombia	85.8	92.2	100.0	103.8	112.1	124.4	107.0	121.0	135.4	136.1
Costa Rica	108.1	104.0	100.0	97.1	96.1	92.5	95.6	91.8	88.4	87.9
Cuba	93.2	102.7	100.0	126.3	132.9	...	...	...	...	...
Dominican Republic	102.2	101.0	100.0	99.0	102.3	97.7	105.7	101.8	96.5	95.5
Ecuador	87.7	89.3	100.0	107.3	110.3	121.1	107.2	118.0	129.8	131.6
El Salvador	101.0	100.0	100.0	98.7	97.7	95.0	98.1	94.4	94.4	93.2
Guatemala	101.9	100.9	100.0	98.1	96.3	93.8	101.8	101.3	100.4	96.1
Haiti	106.8	103.8	100.0	96.2	93.5	67.2	87.0	84.1	69.8	73.5
Honduras	100.9	100.0	100.0	95.4	93.6	87.9	94.0	96.6	104.7	96.7
Mexico	95.4	98.1	100.0	100.5	101.4	102.2	90.8	97.7	104.7	105.3
Nicaragua	103.3	101.4	100.0	97.6	96.6	92.4	101.3	102.2	101.8	101.2
Panama	103.9	101.9	100.0	97.1	96.2	91.8	96.3	94.4	92.4	92.2
Paraguay	104.2	107.1	100.0	98.1	102.7	110.2	107.8	107.8	110.3	113.5
Peru	85.6	93.2	100.0	127.3	132.0	114.4	108.1	127.7	143.9	137.1
Uruguay	114.0	110.1	100.0	97.6	97.8	103.7	106.8	110.2	112.2	114.8
Venezuela (Bolivarian Republic of)	63.9	76.5	100.0	119.4	130.9	161.6	117.6	139.8	168.1	169.7

Source: Economic Commission for Latin America and the Caribbean (ECLAC), on the basis of official figures.
[a] Estimates.

Table A-8
LATIN AMERICA AND THE CARIBBEAN (SELECTED COUNTRIES): REMITTANCES FROM EMIGRANT WORKERS
(Millions of dollars)

	2003	2004	2005	2006	2007	2008	2009	2010	2011	2012 [a]
Brazil	2 018	2 458	2 479	2 890	2 809	2 913	2 224	2 189	2 134	1 497
Colombia	3 060	3 170	3 314	3 890	4 493	4 842	4 145	4 023	4 168	1 993 [b]
Costa Rica	306	302	400	490	596	584	489	505	487	246 [b]
Dominican Republic	2 061	2 230	2 430	2 738	3 046	3 222	3 042	2 998	3 200	1 528 [b]
Ecuador	...	...	...	...	3 335	3 083	2 736	2 591	2 672	1 221 [b]
El Salvador	2 105	2 548	3 017	3 471	3 695	3 742	3 387	3 431	3 649	2 893
Guatemala	2 107	2 551	2 993	3 610	4 128	4 315	3 912	4 127	4 378	3 590
Honduras	842	1 138	1 776	2 329	2 581	2 808	2 476	2 524	2 750	1 398 [b]
Jamaica	...	1 466	1 621	1 770	1 964	2 021	1 792	1 906	2 025	1 520
Mexico	15 139	18 332	21 688	25 567	26 059	25 145	21 306	21 304	22 803	17 267
Nicaragua	439	519	616	698	740	818	768	823	912	741

Source: Economic Commission for Latin America and the Caribbean (ECLAC), on the basis of official figures.
[a] Figures as of September.
[b] Figures as of June.

Table A-9
LATIN AMERICA AND THE CARIBBEAN: NET RESOURCE TRANSFER [a]
(Millions of dollars)

	2003	2004	2005	2006	2007	2008	2009	2010	2011	2012 [b]
Latin America and the Caribbean	**-40 105**	**-67 073**	**-78 398**	**-94 143**	**15 107**	**-32 568**	**-27 114**	**27 195**	**37 709**	**11 149**
Antigua and Barbuda	67	56	136	261	333	291	88	166	83	126
Argentina	-12 535	-7 175	-3 722	-10 388	-198	-14 317	-16 154	-8 573	-16 538	-13 060
Bahamas	431	349	358	1 077	1 037	903	909	622	878	898
Barbados	131	58	263	89	293	204	102	278	372	...
Belize	64	7	25	-51	-84	38	22	-114	-60	-57
Bolivia (Plurinational State of)	-235	-565	-535	-428	-143	-155	-1 162	-906	637	-668
Brazil	-14 234	-29 955	-35 633	-10 553	56 642	-9 401	37 269	56 887	63 799	40 068
Chile	-4 047	-10 615	-10 541	-23 481	-29 153	-1 352	-13 265	-15 011	3 396	-8 992
Colombia	-2 609	-849	-1 846	-2 925	2 713	-788	-2 991	45	-2 055	-1 255
Costa Rica	443	432	1 166	2 058	1 929	2 022	-247	1 097	1 751	1 774
Cuba	-450	150	-633	-618	-960	...	...	...	...	...
Dominica	29	20	62	48	66	103	97	63	68	66
Dominican Republic	-2 787	-2 324	-321	-221	666	2 462	1 248	3 096	2 702	404
Ecuador	-953	-1 084	-1 580	-3 691	-2 138	-2 236	-2 258	-586	-649	525
El Salvador	595	132	-59	375	1 039	1 477	179	-270	24	935
Grenada	87	47	138	203	232	220	155	169	158	180
Guatemala	1 251	1 359	995	1 096	1 179	1 075	-646	92	108	772
Guyana	-6	-10	143	242	215	350	474	414	389	459
Haiti	5	94	-20	201	286	465	479	1 033	589	530
Honduras	94	743	177	149	612	1 530	-428	700	605	684
Jamaica	-246	605	623	798	937	2 120	430	871	1 315	1 587
Mexico	4 128	1 089	727	-10 998	1 098	7 372	-3 498	12 113	20 607	7 685
Nicaragua	520	616	590	804	1 178	1 315	784	830	1 128	1 158
Panama	-539	-414	418	-1 198	925	1 562	-664	1 455	1 727	2 007
Paraguay	168	-98	72	168	400	486	546	439	747	193
Peru	-718	-1 354	-4 596	-7 681	-165	-288	-6 619	3 762	-5 645	5 922
Saint Kitts and Nevis	71	43	23	70	88	157	130	113	111	62
Saint Lucia	115	47	40	268	295	264	102	165	179	234
Saint Vincent and the Grenadines	55	99	70	106	168	204	177	231	176	197
Suriname	118	112	83	-179	-152	-271	-11	-721	-340	-383
Trinidad and Tobago	-1 418	-1 513	-2 878	-7 088	-4 787	-7 016	-3 323	-4 832	-5 345	-4 761
Uruguay	979	-137	84	-52	710	3 045	929	-1 123	2 334	2 456
Venezuela (Bolivarian Republic of)	-8 679	-17 037	-22 225	-22 603	-20 155	-24 408	-19 968	-25 312	-35 543	-28 598

Source: Economic Commission for Latin America and the Caribbean (ECLAC), on the basis of official figures.
[a] The net resource transfer is calculated as total net capital income minus the income balance (net payments of profits and interest). Total net capital income is the balance on the capital and financial accounts plus errors and omissions, plus loans and the use of IMF credit plus exceptional financing. Negative figures indicate resources transferred outside the country.
[b] Estimates.

Table A-10
LATIN AMERICA AND THE CARIBBEAN: NET FOREIGN DIRECT INVESTMENT [a]
(Millions of dollars)

	2003	2004	2005	2006	2007	2008	2009	2010	2011	2012 [b]
Latin America and the Caribbean	**39 790**	**50 212**	**57 309**	**32 519**	**92 803**	**99 425**	**70 740**	**75 004**	**125 851**	**122 486**
Antigua and Barbuda	166	80	221	359	338	174	81	97	59	63
Argentina	878	3 449	3 954	3 099	4 969	8 335	3 307	6 090	7 183	6 401
Bahamas	190	274	563	706	746	860	664	862	667	520
Barbados	58	-16	119	200	256	223	218	...	...	...
Belize	-11	111	126	108	139	167	108	96	93	83
Bolivia (Plurinational State of)	195	83	-291	284	362	508	426	672	859	525
Brazil	9 894	8 339	12 550	-9 380	27 518	24 601	36 033	36 917	67 690	65 612
Chile	2 625	5 096	4 962	5 214	7 720	6 367	5 654	6 351	5 477	4 864
Colombia	783	2 873	5 590	5 558	8 136	8 366	4 049	184	5 546	13 771
Costa Rica	548	733	904	1 371	1 634	2 072	1 339	1 441	2 099	2 200
Dominica	31	26	19	26	40	57	41	24	25	31
Dominican Republic	613	909	1 123	1 085	1 667	2 870	2 165	1 896	2 371	3 771
Ecuador	872	837	493	271	194	1 056	305	161	640	578
El Salvador	123	366	398	268	1 455	824	366	117	385	258
Grenada	89	65	70	90	157	142	103	60	40	66
Guatemala	218	255	470	552	720	737	574	782	967	1 064
Guyana	26	30	77	102	110	178	164	270	308	350
Haiti	14	6	26	161	75	30	38	150	181	124
Honduras	391	553	599	669	926	1 007	505	971	997	1 059
Jamaica	604	542	581	797	751	1 361	480	169	180	...
Mexico	17 301	20 389	17 899	14 248	23 057	25 731	8 940	5 911	8 685	-4 730
Nicaragua	201	250	241	287	382	626	434	508	968	859
Panama	818	1 019	918	2 547	1 899	2 147	1 259	2 350	2 790	2 823
Paraguay	22	32	47	167	178	272	194	340	483	239
Peru	1 275	1 599	2 579	3 467	5 425	6 188	5 165	7 062	8 119	17 874
Saint Kitts and Nevis	76	56	93	110	134	178	131	120	142	69
Saint Lucia	106	77	78	234	272	161	146	110	76	138
Saint Vincent and the Grenadines	55	66	40	109	130	159	97	103	135	110
Suriname	-76	-37	28	-163	-247	-234	-93	-248	73	66
Trinidad and Tobago	583	973	599	513	830	2 101	709	549	1 110	1 688
Uruguay	401	315	811	1 495	1 240	2 117	1 512	2 349	2 629	2 768
Venezuela (Bolivarian Republic of)	722	864	1 422	-2 032	1 587	45	-4 374	-1 462	4 875	-759

Source: Economic Commission for Latin America and the Caribbean (ECLAC), on the basis of official figures.
[a] Corresponds to direct investment in the reporting economy after deduction of outward direct investment by residents of that country. Includes reinvestment of profits.
[b] Estimates. Includes an adjustment due to a lack of data.

Table A-11
LATIN AMERICA AND THE CARIBBEAN: GROSS EXTERNAL DEBT [a]
(Millions of dollars, end-of-period stocks)

		2003	2004	2005	2006	2007	2008	2009	2010	2011	2012 [b]
Latin America and the Caribbean	**Public**	**768 566**	**764 433**	**674 963**	**667 847**	**739 891**	**754 048**	**815 411**	**970 573**	**1 079 898**	**1 104 214**
Antigua and Barbuda	Public	497	532	317	321	481	436	416	431	444	...
Argentina	Total	164 645	171 205	113 768	108 839	124 542	124 916	115 537	129 333	140 655	141 996
Bahamas	Public	364	345	338	334	337	443	767	898	...	...
Barbados	Total	2 475	2 435	2 695	2 991	3 130	3 487	4 009	4 485	...	...
Belize	Public	822	913	970	985	973	958	1 016	1 009	...	...
Bolivia (Plurinational State of)	Total	7 734	7 562	7 666	6 278	5 403	5 930	5 801	5 875	6 298	6 283
Brazil	Total	214 929	201 373	169 451	172 589	193 219	198 340	198 192	256 804	298 204	302 921
Chile	Total	43 067	43 515	46 211	49 497	55 733	64 318	74 041	86 738	98 579	101 875
Colombia	Total	38 065	39 497	38 507	40 103	44 553	46 369	53 719	64 723	75 903	76 255
Costa Rica	Total	5 575	5 766	6 763	7 191	8 444	9 105	8 238	9 189	10 714	11 228
Cuba [c]	Public	11 300	5 806	5 898	7 794	8 908	...	...	...	...	...
Dominica	Public	223	209	221	225	241	234	222	242	248	...
Dominican Republic	Public	5 987	6 380	5 847	6 295	6 556	7 219	8 215	9 947	11 625	12 498
Ecuador	Total	16 756	17 211	17 237	17 099	17 445	16 900	13 514	13 914	15 210	15 017
El Salvador	Total	7 917	8 211	8 877	9 692	9 349	9 994	9 882	9 698	10 670	10 825
Grenada	Public	279	331	401	481	469	481	512	538	514	...
Guatemala	Public	3 467	3 844	3 723	3 958	4 226	4 382	4 928	5 562	5 605	6 238
Guyana	Public	1 199	1 189	1 215	1 043	718	834	933	1 043	1 111	...
Haiti	Public	1 316	1 376	1 335	1 484	1 628	1 917	1 272	353	727	957
Honduras	Total	5 343	6 023	5 135	3 935	3 190	3 464	3 345	3 773	4 188	4 452
Jamaica	Public	4 192	5 120	5 376	5 796	6 123	6 344	6 594	8 390	8 875	6 270
Mexico	Total	132 524	130 925	128 248	119 084	128 090	129 424	165 932	197 727	209 743	218 252
Nicaragua	Public	6 596	5 391	5 348	4 527	3 385	3 512	3 661	3 876	4 073	4 125
Panama	Public	6 504	7 219	7 580	7 788	8 276	8 477	10 150	10 439	10 910	11 005
Paraguay	Total	2 951	2 901	2 700	2 739	2 868	3 256	3 167	3 719	3 817	3 729
Peru	Total	29 587	31 244	28 657	28 897	32 894	34 838	35 157	43 674	47 544	53 881
Saint Kitts and Nevis	Public	316	304	299	310	313	328	306	302	290	...
Saint Lucia	Total	338	369	388	404	415	364	375	393	370	...
Saint Vincent and the Grenadines	Total	195	219	231	220	219	235	261	305	303	...
Suriname	Public	383	384	390	391	298	319	269	334	...	...
Trinidad and Tobago	Public	1 553	1 364	1 329	1 261	1 392	1 445	1 422	1 561	...	...
Uruguay	Total	11 013	11 593	11 418	10 560	12 218	12 021	14 064	14 468	15 024	15 399
Venezuela (Bolivarian Republic of)	Total	40 456	43 679	46 427	44 735	53 855	53 757	69 494	80 831	98 255	101 007

Source: Economic Commission for Latin America and the Caribbean (ECLAC), on the basis of official figures.
[a] Includes debt owed to the International Monetary Fund.
[b] Preliminary figures to June.
[c] As from 2004 refers only to active external debt; excludes other external debt, 60.2% of which is official debt owed to the Paris Club.

Table A-12
LATIN AMERICA AND THE CARIBBEAN: SOVEREIGN SPREADS ON EMBI+ AND EMBI GLOBAL
(Basis points to end of period)

		2003	2004	2005	2006	2007	2008	2009	2010	2011	2012[a]
Argentina	EMBI+	5 632	4 703	504	216	410	1 704	660	496	925	1 066
Belize	EMBI Global	...	...	...	...	591	1 790	1 177	725	1 391	2 325
Brazil	EMBI+	463	382	311	192	221	428	192	189	223	158
Chile	EMBI Global	90	74	80	-84	151	343	95	115	172	126
Colombia	EMBI+	431	332	238	161	195	498	196	172	195	122
Dominican Republic	EMBI Global	996	824	378	196	281	...	...	367	597	348
Ecuador	EMBI+	799	690	669	920	614	4 731	769	913	846	824
El Salvador	EMBI Global	281	245	239	159	199	854	326	323	478	385
Jamaica	EMBI Global	...	...	...	...	384	1 185	719	394	637	681
Mexico	EMBI+	199	166	126	98	149	376	164	149	187	137
Panama	EMBI+	335	290	246	153	201	0	0	162	201	130
Peru	EMBI+	312	220	206	118	178	509	165	163	216	118
Uruguay	EMBI Global	507	327	298	-185	243	685	238	188	213	136
Venezuela (Bolivarian Republic of)	EMBI+	593	411	318	182	506	1 862	1 017	1 044	1 197	926

Source: Economic Commission for Latin America and the Caribbean (ECLAC), on the basis of information from JP Morgan, Emerging Markets Bond Index Monitor.
[a] Figures as of October.

Table A-13
LATIN AMERICA AND THE CARIBBEAN: RISK PREMIA ON FIVE-YEAR CREDIT DEFAULT SWAPS
(Basis points to end of period)

	2003	2004	2005	2006	2007	2008	2009	2010	2011	2012[a]
Argentina	...	...	367	203	462	4 041	914	602	922	1 734
Brazil	404	305	225	100	103	301	123	111	162	112
Chile	54	23	20	19	32	203	68	84	132	81
Colombia	441	341	167	114	130	309	143	113	156	103
Ecuador	...	...	...	849	557	...	...	...	2 300	...
Mexico	122	80	63	41	69	293	134	114	154	102
Panama	282	211	148	81	118	302	134	99	150	103
Peru	292	204	221	91	116	304	124	113	172	104
Venezuela (Bolivarian Republic of)	566	289	221	129	452	3 218	1 104	1 016	928	760

Source: Economic Commission for Latin America and the Caribbean (ECLAC), on the basis of information from Bloomberg.
[a] Figures as of October.

Table A-14
LATIN AMERICA AND THE CARIBBEAN: INTERNATIONAL BOND ISSUES [a]
(Millions of dollars)

	2003	2004	2005	2006	2007	2008	2009	2010	2011	2012 [b]
Latin America and the Caribbean	37 806	36 383	45 188	45 064	41 515	18 913	64 750	90 183	91 687	98 425
National issues	37 806	36 383	44 404	44 247	40 976	18 466	61 950	88 657	89 022	96 037
Argentina	100	200	540	1 896	3 256	65	500	3 146	2 193	663
Bahamas	-	-	-	-	-	100	300	-	-	-
Barbados	-	-	325	215	-	-	450	390	-	-
Bolivia (Plurinational State of)	-	108	-	-	-	-	-	-	-	500
Brazil	19 364	11 603	15 334	19 079	10 608	6 400	25 745	39 305	38 624	46 203
Chile	3 200	2 350	1 000	1 062	250	-	2 773	6 750	6 049	7 200
Colombia	1 545	1 545	2 435	3 177	3 065	1 000	5 450	1 912	6 411	7 459
Costa Rica	490	310	-	-	-	-	-	-	250	250
Dominican Republic	600	-	160	675	605	-	-	1 034	750	-
El Salvador	349	286	375	925	-	-	800	450	654	-
Guatemala	300	380	-	-	-	30	-	-	150	1 400
Honduras	-	-	-	-	-	-	-	20	-	-
Jamaica	-	814	1 050	930	1 900	350	750	1 075	694	1 750
Mexico	7 979	13 312	11 703	9 200	10 296	5 835	15 359	26 882	21 026	24 222
Panama	275	770	1 530	2 076	670	686	1 323	-	897	1 100
Paraguay	-	-	-	-	-	-	-	-	100	200
Peru	1 250	1 305	2 675	733	1 827	-	2 150	4 693	2 155	5 090
Trinidad and Tobago	-	-	100	500	-	-	850	-	175	-
Uruguay	-	350	1 062	3 679	999	-	500	-	1 693	-
Venezuela (Bolivarian Republic of)	2 354	3 050	6 115	100	7 500	4 000	5 000	3 000	7 200	-
Supranational issues	-	-	784	817	539	447	2 800	1 526	2 665	2 388
Central American Bank for Economic Integration	-	-	200	567	-	-	500	151	-	250
Caribbean Development Bank	-	-	-	-	-	-	-	-	175	-
Foreign Trade Bank of Latin America	-	-	-	-	-	-	-	-	-	400
Andean Development Corporation	-	-	584	250	539	447	1 000	1 375	1 240	1 738
NII Holdings	-	-	-	-	-	-	1 300	-	1 250	-

Source: Economic Commission for Latin America and the Caribbean (ECLAC), on the basis of official figures from Merrill-Lynch, JP Morgan and Latin Finance.
[a] Includes sovereign, bank and corporate bonds.
[b] Figures as of October.

Table A-15
LATIN AMERICA AND THE CARIBBEAN: STOCK EXCHANGE INDICES
(National indices to end of period, 31 December 2005=100)

	2003	2004	2005	2006	2007	2008	2009	2010	2011	2012 [a]
Argentina	69	89	100	135	139	70	150	228	160	151
Brazil	66	78	100	133	191	112	205	207	170	171
Chile	76	91	100	137	155	121	182	251	213	217
Colombia	25	46	100	117	112	79	122	163	133	155
Costa Rica	87	78	100	177	217	207	142	118	121	130
Ecuador	65	79	100	130	121	128	107	126	128	136
Jamaica	65	108	100	96	103	77	80	82	91	86
Mexico	49	73	100	149	166	126	180	217	208	234
Peru	51	77	100	268	365	147	295	487	406	433
Trinidad and Tobago	65	101	100	91	92	79	72	78	95	102
Venezuela (Bolivarian Republic of)	109	147	100	256	186	172	270	320	574	1 766

Source: Economic Commission for Latin America and the Caribbean (ECLAC), on the basis of information from Bloomberg.
[a] Figures as of October.

Table A-16
LATIN AMERICA AND THE CARIBBEAN: GROSS INTERNATIONAL RESERVES
(Millions of dollars, end-of-period stocks)

	2003	2004	2005	2006	2007	2008	2009	2010	2011	2012[a]
Latin America and the Caribbean	**197 847**	**225 943**	**262 402**	**319 242**	**459 464**	**512 611**	**567 421**	**655 993**	**774 230**	**829 390**
Antigua and Barbuda [b]	114	120	127	143	144	138	108	136	147	178[c]
Argentina	13 820	19 299	27 262	31 167	45 711	46 198	47 967	52 145	46 376	45 274
Bahamas	484	668	579	500	454	563	816	861	897	757[d]
Barbados	752	595	618	597	775	680	829	805	805	751[e]
Belize	...	...	...	95	99	156	210	216	242	272[d]
Bolivia (Plurinational State of)	1 096	1 272	1 798	3 193	5 319	7 722	8 580	9 730	12 018	13 772
Brazil	49 296	52 935	53 799	85 839	180 334	193 783	238 520	288 575	352 012	377 753
Chile	15 851	16 016	16 963	19 429	16 910	23 162	25 371	27 864	41 979	38 943
Colombia	10 608	13 220	14 634	15 109	20 607	23 672	24 992	28 464	32 303	36 402
Costa Rica [f]	1 839	1 922	2 313	3 115	4 114	3 799	4 066	4 627	4 756	5 366
Dominica [b]	48	42	49	63	60	55	64	66	74	84[c]
Dominican Republic [f]	279	825	1 929	2 251	2 946	2 662	3 307	3 765	4 098	3 347
Ecuador [g]	...	...	2 147	2 023	3 521	4 473	3 792	2 622	2 958	4 033
El Salvador	1 910	1 893	1 833	1 908	2 198	2 545	2 987	2 883	2 504	2 519
Grenada [b]	83	122	94	100	110	104	112	103	105	105[c]
Guatemala [f]	2 932	3 529	3 783	4 061	4 310	4 659	5 213	5 954	6 188	6 804
Guyana	272	225	251	277	313	356	628	780	798	827[e]
Haiti	112	166	187	305	494	587	733	1 283	1 343	1 400[e]
Honduras [f]	1 609	2 159	2 526	2 824	2 733	2 690	2 174	2 775	2 880	2 524[d]
Jamaica	1 196	1 882	2 169	2 399	1 906	1 795	1 752	2 979	2 820	1 990
Mexico	59 028	64 198	74 110	76 330	87 211	95 302	99 893	120 587	149 209	165 590[d]
Nicaragua	504	670	730	924	1 103	1 141	1 573	1 799	1 892	1 856
Panama [f]	1 046	699	1 245	1 379	2 094	2 637	3 222	2 843	2 514	1 971[d]
Paraguay	983	1 168	1 293	1 703	2 462	2 864	3 861	4 169	4 984	4 838[d]
Peru	10 206	12 649	14 120	17 329	27 720	31 233	33 175	44 150	48 859	62 212
Saint Kitts and Nevis [b]	65	78	71	89	96	110	123	156	232	259[c]
Saint Lucia [b]	105	130	114	132	151	140	151	182	190	192[c]
Saint Vincent and the Grenadines [b]	50	74	69	78	86	83	75	111	88	91[c]
Suriname [h]	106	129	126	215	401	433	659	639	941	970
Trinidad and Tobago	...	2 539	4 015	5 134	6 674	9 380	8 652	9 070	9 823	9 326[e]
Uruguay	2 087	2 512	3 078	3 091	4 121	6 360	7 987	7 743	10 302	13 120
Venezuela (Bolivarian Republic of)	21 366	24 208	30 368	37 440	34 286	43 127	35 830	27 911	29 892	25 864

Source: Economic Commission for Latin America and the Caribbean (ECLAC), on the basis of official figures.
[a] Figures as of October.
[b] Net international reserves.
[c] Figures as of March.
[d] Figures as of September.
[e] Figures as of August.
[f] Serie corresponding to the harmonized monetary and financial statistics.
[g] Freely available International reserves.
[h] Does not include gold.

Table A-17
LATIN AMERICA AND THE CARIBBEAN: REAL EFFECTIVE EXCHANGE RATES [a]
(Indices: 2005=100, average values for the period)

	2003	2004	2005	2006	2007	2008	2009	2010	2011 [b]	2012 [b] [c]
Latin America and the Caribbean [d]	**107.1**	**106.8**	**100.0**	**97.3**	**94.3**	**88.5**	**87.9**	**85.0**	**82.8**	**80.7**
Argentina	96.9	100.2	100.0	101.9	101.4	97.2	99.3	98.5	99.5	94.8
Barbados	97.9	101.4	100.0	97.4	98.2	97.7	86.8	89.3	86.0	83.2
Bolivia (Plurinational State of)	86.9	92.6	100.0	102.3	101.3	92.5	84.3	88.1	86.9	82.4
Brazil	128.9	122.6	100.0	89.0	82.5	79.9	81.5	70.6	67.2	74.3
Chile	113.1	105.6	100.0	95.5	97.2	96.9	100.9	95.4	94.5	92.7
Colombia	124.5	113.1	100.0	101.9	91.5	87.9	91.9	79.8	80.5	77.0
Costa Rica	96.8	99.4	100.0	99.1	96.5	93.4	91.8	81.7	79.6	77.0
Dominica	94.5	97.2	100.0	101.8	104.7	105.5	108.1	106.8	110.1	112.0
Dominican Republic	145.1	139.0	100.0	106.0	106.1	108.6	110.4	108.8	110.1	112.0
Ecuador	92.0	96.1	100.0	101.4	107.0	108.7	101.9	100.1	102.3	99.7
El Salvador	98.2	98.5	100.0	100.7	101.7	103.0	100.4	101.9	102.8	102.9
Guatemala	111.7	108.5	100.0	97.1	96.6	91.7	94.6	94.2	90.4	88.8
Honduras	98.5	100.2	100.0	98.7	97.5	93.8	87.0	85.9	85.1	83.7
Jamaica	109.7	107.7	100.0	102.1	105.0	99.2	111.1	98.5	96.2	96.0
Mexico	99.9	103.7	100.0	100.0	100.8	103.3	117.9	108.9	108.9	112.8
Nicaragua	97.3	99.0	100.0	99.6	100.3	97.6	103.7	101.2	106.2	108.0
Panama	93.6	99.9	100.0	101.7	103.2	101.5	97.0	98.1	98.2	94.2
Paraguay	95.8	92.3	100.0	88.5	81.6	72.9	80.3	77.9	69.7	70.9
Peru	98.4	99.4	100.0	101.9	102.6	99.3	97.7	94.1	95.9	89.3
Trinidad and Tobago	98.1	100.3	100.0	96.6	94.8	90.7	82.6	78.2	78.8	73.3
Uruguay	109.8	111.8	100.0	99.1	98.8	91.5	90.7	78.7	76.6	75.1
Venezuela (Bolivarian Republic of)	97.7	98.2	100.0	93.3	83.1	67.4	51.2	77.9	68.1	57.5

Source: Economic Commission for Latin America and the Caribbean (ECLAC), on the basis of official figures from the International Monetary Fund and national sources.
[a] A country's overall real effective exchange rate index is calculated by weighting its real bilateral exchange rate indices with each of its trading partners by each partner's share in the country's total trade flows in terms of exports and imports. The extraregional real effective exchange rate index excludes trade with other Latin American and Caribbean countries. A currency depreciates in real effective terms when this index rises and appreciates when it falls.
[b] Preliminary figures, weighted by trade in 2010.
[c] Figures as of October.
[d] Simple average of the extraregional real effective exchange rate for 20 countries.

Table A-18
LATIN AMERICA AND THE CARIBBEAN: PARTICIPATION RATE
(Average annual rates)

		2003	2004	2005	2006	2007	2008	2009	2010	2011	2011	2012 [a]
											January to October	
Latin America and the Caribbean [b]		**61.7**	**61.7**	**61.2**	**61.4**	**61.5**	**61.8**	**61.9**	**61.6**	**61.7**	...	...
Argentina	Urban areas	60.2	60.2	59.9	60.3	59.5	58.8	59.3	58.9	59.5	59.6	59.2 [c]
Barbados	Nationwide total	69.3	69.4	69.6	67.9	67.8	67.6	67.0	66.6	67.6	68.1	66.7 [d]
Bolivia (Plurinational State of)	Departamental capitals [e]	67.6	64.9	62.8	66.3	64.8 l	...	56.9	57.3	...	...	...
Brazil	Six metropolitan areas	57.1	57.2	56.6	56.9	56.9	57.0	56.7	57.1	57.1	57.1	57.2
Chile [f]	Nationwide total	54.4	55.0	55.6	54.8	54.9	56.0	55.9 l	58.5	59.8	59.8	59.6 [c]
Colombia	Nationwide total	62.9	61.5	60.5	59.1	58.3	58.5	61.3	62.7	63.7	63.4	64.6
Costa Rica [g]	Nationwide total	55.5	54.4	56.8	56.6	57.0	56.7 l	60.4	59.1	60.7	60.7	60.1 [h]
Cuba [i]	Nationwide total	70.9	71.0	72.1	72.1	73.7	74.7	75.4	74.9	76.1	...	...
Dominican Republic	Nationwide total	54.7	56.3	55.9	56.0	56.1	55.6	53.8	55.0	56.2	56.2	56.5 [j]
Ecuador	Urban total	58.2	59.1	59.5	59.1	61.3	60.1	58.9	56.9	55.2	55.1	56.3 [c]
El Salvador [k]	Nationwide total	53.4	51.7	52.4	52.6 l	62.1	62.7	62.8	62.5	62.7	...	...
Honduras	Nationwide total	50.0	50.6	50.9	50.7	50.7	51.0	53.1	53.6	51.9	...	...
Jamaica	Nationwide total	64.4	64.3	64.2	64.7	64.9	65.4	63.5	62.4	62.3	62.4	62.4 l
Mexico	Nationwide total	57.1	57.7	57.9	58.8	58.8	58.7	58.6	58.4	58.6	58.6	59.3
Nicaragua [g]	Nationwide total	53.7	53.1	53.8	51.4	53.4	53.3 l	66.9	72.1	...	...	...
Panama	Nationwide total	62.8	63.3	63.6	62.6	62.7	63.9	64.1	63.5	61.9	61.9	63.5 [m]
Paraguay	Nationwide total [n]	59.8	63.4	61.8	59.4	60.8	61.7	62.9	60.5	60.7 l	62.2	62.7 [c]
Peru	Metropolitan Lima	67.4	68.0	67.1	67.4	68.9	68.1	68.4	70.0	70.0	70.0	69.2 [c]
Trinidad and Tobago	Nationwide total	61.6	63.0	63.7	63.9	63.5	63.5	62.7	62.1	61.3	...	...
Uruguay	Nationwide total [o]	58.1	58.5	58.5 l	60.8	62.7	62.5	63.2	62.9	63.9	64.0	63.3
Venezuela (Bolivarian Republic of)	Nationwide total	69.3	68.5	66.3	65.4	64.9	64.9	65.1	64.6	64.4	64.4	64.0

Source: Economic Commission for Latin America and the Caribbean (ECLAC), on the basis of official figures.
[a] The figures in the last two columns refer to the period January-October.
[b] The data relating to the different countries are not comparable owing to differences in coverage and in the definition of the working age population.
The regional series are simple averages of national data (excluding Nicaragua and the Plurinational State of Bolivia) and include adjustments for lack of information and changes in methodology.
[c] The figures in the last two columns refer to the period January-September.
[d] The figures in the last two columns refer to the period January-June.
[e] Up to 2007, urban areas.
[f] New measurements have been used since 2010; the data are not comparable with the previous series.
[g] New measurements have been used since 2009; the data are not comparable with the previous series.
[h] The figures in the last two columns refer to the measurement of July.
[i] The working-age population is measured as follows: for males, 17 to 59 years and for females, 15 to 54 years.
[j] The figures in the last two columns refer to the measurement of April.
[k] New measurements have been used since 2007; the data are not comparable with the previous series.
[l] The figures in the last two columns refer to the period January-July.
[m] The figures in the last two columns refer to the measurement of August.
[n] The figures in the last two columns refer to Asunción and urban areas of the Departamento Central.
[o] Up to 2005, urban total.

Table A-19
LATIN AMERICA AND THE CARIBBEAN: OPEN URBAN UNEMPLOYMENT [a]
(Average annual rates)

		2003	2004	2005	2006	2007	2008	2009	2010	2011	2012 [b]
Latin America and the Caribbean [c]		**11.1**	**10.3**	**9.0**	**8.6**	**7.9**	**7.3**	**8.1**	**7.3**	**6.7**	**6.4**
Argentina	Urban areas	17.3	13.6	11.6	10.2	8.5	7.9	8.7	7.7	7.2	7.3 [d]
Bahamas [e]	Nationwide total	10.8	10.2	10.2	7.6	7.9	8.7	14.2	...	13.7	...
Barbados [e]	Nationwide total	11.0	9.8	9.1	8.7	7.4	8.1	10.0	10.8	11.2	12.2 [f]
Belize [e]	Nationwide total	12.9	11.6	11.0	9.4	8.5	8.2	13.1	...	...	...
Bolivia (Plurinational State of)	Departamental capitals [g]	9.2	6.2	8.1	8.0	7.7	6.7 l	7.9	6.1	5.8	...
Brazil	Six metropolitan areas	12.3	11.5	9.8	10.0	9.3	7.9	8.1	6.7	6.0	5.5
Chile [h]	Nationwide total	9.5	10.0	9.2	7.7	7.1	7.8	9.7 l	8.2	7.1	6.4
Colombia [e]	Thirteen metropolitan areas	17.1	15.8	14.3	13.1	11.4	11.5	13.0	12.4	11.5	11.3
Colombia [i]	Thirteen metropolitan areas	15.7	14.4	13.1	12.2	10.7	11.0	12.4	11.8	10.9	10.7
Costa Rica [j]	Urban total	6.7	6.7	6.9	6.0	4.8	4.8 l	8.5	7.1	7.7	7.8
Cuba	Nationwide total	2.3	1.9	1.9	1.9	1.8	1.6	1.7	2.5	3.2	...
Dominican Republic [e]	Nationwide total	16.7	18.4	17.9	16.2	15.6	14.1	14.9	14.3	14.6	14.3 [k]
Dominican Republic [i]	Nationwide total	6.8	6.1	6.4	5.5	5.1	4.7	5.3	5.5	6.4	6.4 [k]
Ecuador [e]	Urban total	11.6	9.7	8.5	8.1	7.4	6.9	8.5	7.6	6.0	4.8 [d]
Ecuador [i]	Urban total	8.4	7.0	6.5	5.7	5.5	5.3	6.8	6.1	4.9	4.3 [d]
El Salvador	Urban total	6.2	6.5	7.3	5.7	5.8	5.5	7.1	6.8	6.6	...
Guatemala	Urban total	5.4	4.4	...	...	...	...	...	4.8	3.1	2.7
Honduras	Urban total	7.6	8.0	6.5	4.9	4.0	4.1	4.9	6.4	6.8	...
Jamaica [e][h]	Nationwide total	11.4	11.7	11.3	10.3	9.8	10.6	11.4 l	12.4	12.6	13.7 [l]
Jamaica [i][h]	Nationwide total	5.3	6.4	5.8	5.8	6.0	6.9	7.5 l	8.0	8.3	9.0 [l]
Mexico	Urban areas	4.6	5.3	4.7	4.6	4.8	4.9	6.7	6.4	6.0	5.8
Nicaragua	Urban total	10.2	9.3	7.0	7.0	6.9	8.0	10.5	9.7	...	...
Panama [e]	Urban total	15.9	14.1	12.1	10.4	7.8	6.5	7.9	7.7	5.4	4.8 [m]
Panama [i]	Urban total	13.7	11.4	9.8	8.4	5.8	5.0	6.3	5.8	3.6	3.6 [m]
Paraguay	Urban total	11.2	10.0	7.6	8.9	7.2	7.4	8.2	7.0	6.5	...
Peru	Metropolitan Lima	9.4	9.4	9.6	8.5	8.4	8.4	8.4	7.9	7.7	7.0
Trinidad and Tobago	Nationwide total	10.5	8.4	8.0	6.2	5.6	4.6	5.3	5.9	5.1	...
Uruguay	Urban total	16.9	13.1	12.2	11.4	9.6	7.9	7.6	7.1	6.3	6.2
Venezuela (Bolivarian Republic of)	Nationwide total	18.0	15.3	12.4	9.9	8.4	7.3	7.9	8.7	8.3	8.0

Source: Economic Commission for Latin America and the Caribbean (ECLAC), on the basis of household surveys.
[a] Unemployed population as a percentage of the economically active population.
[b] Estimates based on data from January to October.
[c] Weighted average adjusted for lack of information and differences and changes in methodology.
   The data relating to the different countries are not comparable owing to differences in coverage and in the definition of the working age population.
[d] Estimate based on data from January to September.
[e] Includes hidden unemployment.
[f] Promedio de enero a junio. January-June average.
[g] Up to 2008, urban areas.
[h] New measurements have been used since 2010; the data are not comparable with the previous series.
[i] Excluye el desempleo oculto. Incluye un ajuste a las cifras de población económicamente activa.
[j] New measurements have been used since 2009; the data are not comparable with the previous series.
[k] Figure for April.
[l] Promedio de enero a julio. January-July average.
[m] Figure for August.

Table A-20
LATIN AMERICA AND THE CARIBBEAN: EMPLOYMENT RATE[a]
(Average annual rates)

		2003	2004	2005	2006	2007	2008	2009	2010	2011	2011	2012[b]
											January to October	
Latin America and the Caribbean[c]		**52.4**	**52.9**	**53.3**	**53.7**	**54.2**	**54.5**	**54.2**	**54.9**	**55.4**	...	...
Argentina	Urban total	49.8	52.0	52.9	54.1	54.5	54.2	54.2	54.4	55.2	55.2	54.9[d]
Bahamas	Nationwide total	69.7	68.0	68.5	69.4	70.2	69.7	63.0	...	62.4	...	...
Barbados	Nationwide total	61.6	62.7	63.2	61.9	62.7	62.1	60.3	59.4	60.0	60.5	58.6[e]
Bolivia (Plurinational State of)	Departamental capitals[f]	54.9	55.0	51.2	54.0	52.7 l	...	52.4	53.6	...	...	...
Brazil	Six metropolitan areas	50.1	50.6	51.0	51.2	51.6	52.5	52.1	53.2	53.7	53.6	54.0
Chile[g]	Nationwide total	49.3	49.5	50.4	50.5	51.0	51.7	50.5 l	53.7	55.5	55.5	55.6[d]
Colombia	Nationwide total	54.1	53.1	53.4	52.0	51.8	51.9	53.9	55.4	56.8	56.3	57.8
Costa Rica[h]	Nationwide total	51.8	50.9	53.0	53.3	54.4	53.9 l	55.4	54.8	56.0	56.0	55.4[i]
Cuba[j]	Nationwide total	69.2	69.7	70.7	70.7	72.4	73.6	74.2	73.0	73.6	...	...
Dominican Republic	Nationwide total	45.4	46.0	45.9	46.9	47.4	47.7	45.8	47.1	48.0	48.0	48.4[k]
Ecuador	Urban total	51.5	53.5	54.4	54.3	56.8	56.0	53.9	52.6	51.9	51.6	53.6[d]
El Salvador[l]	Nationwide total	49.7	48.2	48.3	49.2 l	58.1	59.0	58.2	58.1	58.6	...	...
Honduras	Nationwide total	47.4	48.6	48.6	49.0	49.2	49.4	51.5	51.5	49.7	...	...
Jamaica[g]	Nationwide total	57.1	56.8	57.0	58.0	58.6	58.5	56.3 l	54.6	54.4	54.5	54.1[m]
Mexico	Nationwide total	55.3	55.4	55.8	56.7	56.7	56.3	55.4	55.3	55.6	55.4	56.4
Nicaragua[h]	Nationwide total	49.5	49.6	50.8	48.8	48.6	50.1 l	61.8	66.8	...	...	...
Panama	Nationwide total	54.6	55.9	57.3	57.2	58.7	60.3	59.9	59.4	59.1	59.1	61.0[n]
Paraguay	Nationwide total[o]	55.0	58.8	58.2	55.4	57.4	58.2	58.9	57.1	57.3 l	57.5	57.6
Peru	Metropolitana Lima	61.1	61.6	60.7	61.8	63.0	62.4	62.7	64.5	64.5	64.4	64.2[d]
Trinidad and Tobago	Nationwide total	55.2	57.8	58.6	59.9	59.9	60.6	59.4	58.4	58.2	...	...
Uruguay	Nationwide total[p]	48.3	50.9	51.4 l	54.2	56.8	57.7	58.5	59.0	60.0	60.0	59.5
Venezuela (Bolivarian Republic of)	Nationwide total	56.8	58.1	58.1	58.9	59.4	60.2	60.0	59.0	59.0	58.8	58.8

Source: Economic Commission for Latin America and the Caribbean (ECLAC), on the basis of official figures.
[a] Employed population as a percentage of the working-age population.
[b] The figures in the last two columns refer to the period January-October.
[c] Weighted average adjusted for lack of information and differences and changes in methodology.
  The data relating to the different countries are not comparable owing to differences in coverage and in the definition of the working age population.
[d] The figures in the last two columns refer to the period January-September.
[e] The figures in the last two columns refer to the period January-June.
[f] Up to 2007, urban areas.
[g] New measurements have been used since 2010; the data are not comparable with the previous series.
[h] New measurements have been used since 2009; the data are not comparable with the previous series.
[i] The figures in the last two columns refer to the measurement of July.
[j] The working-age population is measured as follows: for males, 17 to 59 years and for females, 15 to 54 years.
[k] The figures in the last two columns refer to the measurement of April.
[l] New measurements have been used since 2007; the data are not comparable with the previous series.
[m] The figures in the last two columns refer to the period January-July.
[n] The figures in the last two columns refer to the measurement of August.
[o] The figures in the last two columns refer to Asunción and urban areas of the Departamento Central.
[p] Up to 2005, urban total.

Table A-21
LATIN AMERICA: REAL AVERAGE WAGES [a]
(Indices 2005=100)

	2003	2004	2005	2006	2007	2008	2009	2010	2011	2012[b]
Argentina [c]	85.2	93.1	100.0	108.9	118.8	129.2	144.3	163.0	196.1	231.8[d]
Bolivia (Plurinational State of) [e]	101.0	103.7	100.0	92.0	86.8	80.1	81.9	84.5	83.4	...
Brazil [f]	99.6	100.4	100.0	103.5	105.0	107.2	108.6	110.9	113.6	117.7[d]
Chile [g]	96.4	98.1	100.0	101.9	104.8	104.6	109.6l	112.0	114.8	118.5[d]
Colombia [h]	96.9	98.8	100.0	104.0	103.8	102.3	103.6	106.4	106.5	107.5[d]
Costa Rica [i]	104.7	101.9	100.0	101.6	102.9	100.9	108.6	110.9	117.2	119.0
Cuba	83.2	88.5	100.0	111.6	109.9	110.0	115.1	118.5	118.8	...
El Salvador [j]	106.1	102.4	100.0	100.4	98.0	94.9	98.2	99.3	96.4	...
Guatemala [i]	106.5	104.2	100.0	98.9	97.3	94.8	94.9	97.6	98.0	...
Mexico [i]	96.5	98.1	100.0	101.6	103.1	103.3	102.3	101.4	102.2	102.3
Nicaragua [i]	102.0	99.8	100.0	101.4	99.6	95.9	101.5	102.8	102.9	103.1
Panama	102.0	101.2	100.0	102.0	103.4	99.1	101.8	103.7	109.2	113.5[k]
Paraguay	97.3	99.0	100.0	100.6	103.0	102.3	106.8	107.6	110.6	110.9[l]
Peru [m]	100.9	102.0	100.0	101.2	99.4	101.6	104.8	107.5	...	...
Uruguay	95.6	95.6	100.0	104.3	109.3	113.2	121.4	125.5	130.5	135.7
Venezuela (Bolivarian Republic of)	97.2	97.5	100.0	105.1	106.4	101.5	94.8	89.9	92.5	97.5[d]

Source: Economic Commission for Latin America and the Caribbean (ECLAC), on the basis of official figures.
[a] Figures deflated by the official consumer price index of each country.
[b] Estimates based on data from January to October.
[c] Registered private-sector workers.
[d] Estimate based on data from January to September.
[e] Private-sector average wage index.
[f] Private-sector workers covered by social and labour legislation.
[g] General index of hourly remuneration. New measurements have been used since 2010; the data are not comparable with the previous series.
[h] Manufacturing.
[i] Average wage declared by workers covered by social security.
[j] Gross salary.
[k] Estimate based on data from January to June.
[l] Figure for June.
[m] Private-sector workers in the Lima metropolitan area.

Table A-22
LATIN AMERICA AND THE CARIBBEAN: MONETARY
(Percentage variation with respect to the year-earlier period)

		2003	2004	2005	2006	2007	2008	2009	2010	2011	2012 [a]
Antigua and Barbuda	Monetary base	13.0	6.8	17.2	4.2	10.0	2.0	-10.5	0.9	20.1	...
	Money (M1)	4.3	34.8	28.8	10.8	16.4	6.7	-14.2	-7.3	-6.6	-1.1 [b]
	M2	16.1	16.0	10.4	7.2	11.3	7.6	-2.9	-3.1	-1.1	2.0
	Foreign-currency deposits	9.5	15.5	30.4	15.9	32.0	-0.5	45.4	-1.8	3.2	-6.3
Argentina	Monetary base	69.5	28.2	10.5	23.7	29.0	19.1	5.4	25.1	37.1	34.0
	Money (M1)	40.8	37.2	27.0	23.8	27.2	17.4	7.7	27.1	58.6	31.5 [c]
	M2	29.9	25.3	24.4	21.6	26.3	18.6	3.0	29.3	49.3	30.8
	Foreign-currency deposits	51.2	143.8	21.2	37.9	27.8	36.4	61.6	35.9	8.7	-22.1
Bahamas	Monetary base	7.3	31.9	-8.1	-3.0	17.2	6.4	2.0	2.5	26.8	-8.1 [c]
	Money (M1)	4.3	24.0	16.0	3.2	1.5	0.3	-0.2	2.8	6.2	8.4
	M2	1.9	9.2	8.9	7.1	8.5	6.5	2.8	2.8	2.3	1.3
	Foreign-currency deposits	13.2	1.7	22.6	13.8	17.7	15.9	8.4	0.1	-2.7	11.1
Barbados	Monetary base	15.8	-3.3	-15.8	4.8	26.8	9.2	-13.9	3.4	7.7	-5.8 [b]
	Money (M1)	19.5	23.4	6.0	4.1	11.9	7.5	-5.4	2.2	-1.0	-22.6 [d]
	M2	7.7	15.5	8.8	11.0	15.8	8.7	-1.1	-1.1	-0.4	-9.6
Belize	Monetary base	-1.1	3.4	19.3	19.2	15.1	11.5	11.9	-1.2	8.2	17.8 [c]
	Money (M1)	12.0	14.8	7.3	13.0	17.0	9.2	-1.9	-0.9	9.1	22.9 [c]
Bolivia (Plurinational State of)	Monetary base	10.5	5.0	27.4	44.3	48.2	53.8	19.6	32.4	11.6	20.4 [b]
	Money (M1)	15.2	15.7	31.4	45.1	55.2	50.2	9.4	24.1	27.2	18.9 [b]
	M2	16.7	19.4	39.8	53.6	68.1	59.6	18.4	34.6	34.0	32.8
	Foreign-currency deposits	4.1	-4.6	4.8	-2.8	11.2	-9.2	20.4	4.7	-12.8	-4.7
Brazil	Monetary base	17.1	10.7	15.3	18.6	20.9	12.5	8.0	17.5	11.0	9.0
	Money (M1)	7.0	18.9	13.8	15.4	23.3	11.8	7.5	17.3	6.2	4.3
	M2	11.1	12.8	18.4	15.6	14.1	30.3	22.2	11.0	21.0	14.2
Chile	Monetary base	6.4	12.6	17.0	15.8	20.5	10.3	11.8	17.7	14.7	14.6
	Money (M1)	19.3	21.2	14.0	11.9	17.9	12.0	13.1	28.7	11.3	10.6
	M2	3.1	8.1	20.8	19.1	20.2	19.1	2.5	3.9	13.2	20.3
	Foreign-currency deposits	4.0	3.6	1.6	17.4	11.5	47.3	-0.6	6.5	13.0	8.6
Colombia	Monetary base	16.3	16.6	19.6	23.2	18.1	14.3	10.3	12.4	15.1	9.9
	Money (M1)	16.0	15.1	18.5	20.6	13.5	8.0	9.8	14.7	16.2	7.1
	M2	11.3	14.0	20.1	18.0	18.7	14.6	13.2	6.9	14.8	17.2 [c]
Costa Rica	Monetary base	27.2	22.1	27.2	30.2	25.4	25.7	6.3	10.0	11.7	10.7 [c]
	Money (M1)	16.4	14.4	18.1	25.2	41.1	21.7	-3.4	9.4	19.4	9.1 [c]
	M2	23.4	16.6	28.4	29.9	34.9	22.9	1.3	2.6	11.1	13.4
	Foreign-currency deposits	22.5	34.5	24.5	17.0	7.2	10.7	36.8	-1.9	-5.4	-0.5
Dominica	Monetary base	-3.6	12.5	-10.5	9.9	6.5	-0.1	-4.6	9.7	8.5	...
	Money (M1)	5.1	30.4	24.7	10.8	10.1	4.4	-1.3	-1.5	-2.1	8.1 [b]
	M2	3.5	14.1	13.4	6.7	10.5	8.2	7.5	3.8	3.2	6.3
	Foreign-currency deposits	-44.7	149.5	-33.2	-32.1	-0.6	19.0	15.9	30.2	38.8	22.7
Dominican Republic	Monetary base	56.0	32.4	9.0	13.2	18.4	12.3	3.4	6.4	5.8	9.1
	Money (M1)	58.0	35.0	5.6	29.7	26.7	11.0	-1.1	17.7	4.9	6.5
	M2	53.2	36.8	13.0	0.0	14.2	10.6	7.2	13.3	8.8	12.4
	Foreign-currency deposits	103.2	26.7	-7.8	16.9	11.0	14.9	4.6	18.7	17.8	19.0
Ecuador	Monetary base	...	...	...	...	...	16.4	18.1	24.1	9.9	14.0 [d]
	Money (M1)	...	...	...	...	...	44.5	38.0	16.1	15.5	13.3 [d]
	M2	...	...	...	...	...	33.0	22.0	18.6	20.0	19.1
El Salvador	Monetary base	3.9	5.4	-4.4	7.1	13.9	8.1	10.8	0.4	-1.3	2.6 [c]
	Money (M1)	0.1	11.0	9.7	12.6	12.2	8.5	7.6	19.8	10.4	6.0 [c]
	M2	0.8	2.6	3.1	9.1	15.0	6.1	0.9	1.6	-2.1	0.4
Grenada	Monetary base	9.0	19.9	0.1	-11.1	9.2	3.5	-8.5	6.0	7.2	...
	Money (M1)	12.2	36.6	18.6	-5.8	7.1	3.1	-12.9	3.8	-7.3	2.1 [b]
	M2	7.4	15.9	10.9	-0.9	5.2	8.1	1.0	3.4	0.4	1.6
	Foreign-currency deposits	16.4	1.6	4.2	-18.7	26.0	2.7	17.4	-3.9	-5.5	13.5
Guatemala	Monetary base	10.8	8.1	12.3	18.9	17.3	4.1	6.6	8.0	10.1	4.5
	Money (M1)	13.9	10.4	15.1	17.9	17.6	3.4	7.6	7.2	9.1	5.5
	M2	10.0	8.6	13.5	19.9	11.7	7.3	9.4	8.4	10.6	9.2
	Foreign-currency deposits	92.9	298.7	6.8	6.1	4.2	9.9	18.1	11.6	4.9	2.7
Guyana	Monetary base	9.3	9.1	12.3	4.2	0.8	16.5	10.6	17.7	17.4	14.1 [c]
	Money (M1)	7.5	19.8	10.0	14.2	20.5	18.6	8.2	12.9	21.9	15.9 [c]

Table A-22 (concluded)

		2003	2004	2005	2006	2007	2008	2009	2010	2011	2012 [a]
Haiti	Monetary base	34.5	20.2	10.9	12.4	11.3	16.1	14.2	34.1	18.1	7.3 [b]
	Money (M1)	28.7	12.5	15.2	8.8	3.5	21.3	9.2	27.0	14.4	5.7 [b]
	M2	29.1	15.5	11.1	9.6	5.3	13.7	6.9	17.4	10.0	3.8
	Foreign-currency deposits	59.7	11.5	17.6	15.9	3.2	22.1	14.4	22.5	18.4	7.2
Honduras	Monetary base	2.8	19.0	21.0	14.9	31.3	24.8	11.6	-13.8	10.7	12.8 [c]
	Money (M1)	13.7	13.8	14.6	22.0	18.4	11.5	2.2	5.2	17.7	4.7 [c]
	M2	11.3	13.6	17.1	26.5	19.4	9.2	0.8	4.7	17.1	9.2
	Foreign-currency deposits	9.2	15.8	20.5	12.7	10.5	20.3	-1.0	5.4	7.8	14.4
Jamaica	Monetary base	7.4	13.2	9.1	14.2	15.1	9.5	22.8	5.5	5.3	6.1
	Money (M1)	3.5	20.6	14.7	17.2	18.8	9.1	7.6	7.0	7.8	4.3 [b]
	M2	2.3	13.7	11.5	11.8	14.3	7.9	4.4	6.1	5.6	3.0
	Foreign-currency deposits	33.6	21.4	7.3	3.0	18.2	10.9	17.5	-0.9	-4.8	4.8
Mexico	Monetary base	15.7	14.0	12.1	16.5	12.6	12.6	15.9	9.7	9.5	14.4
	Money (M1)	13.2	12.3	12.9	35.9	11.6	8.5	11.8	11.2	16.2	14.6
	M2	12.1	6.9	11.6	19.8	7.5	13.9	11.5	5.8	12.4	11.0
	Foreign-currency deposits	-4.4	13.5	10.9	24.9	-6.4	2.8	20.7	0.9	3.0	16.2
Nicaragua	Monetary base	14.0	25.7	21.3	25.5	18.3	15.2	0.7	24.0	20.5	19.3 [c]
	Money (M1)	11.1	25.5	23.3	18.8	18.2	32.9	4.4	21.4	24.8	21.4 [c]
	M2	11.1	25.5	23.3	18.8	18.2	32.9	4.4	21.4	24.8	21.4
	Foreign-currency deposits	9.6	13.5	12.5	10.5	8.0	10.2	5.3	25.8	7.8	21.5
Panama	Monetary base	-15.6	10.4	12.7	7.5	9.6	17.7	11.2	7.5	27.1	11.8 [c]
	Money (M1)	-4.2	15.2	9.5	24.5	29.2	26.5	17.4	19.2	21.5	17.5 [c]
	M2	-0.5	8.0	5.5	14.8	22.4	17.1	9.2	11.3	9.9	10.5
Paraguay	Monetary base	41.3	35.0	2.3	8.7	31.2	27.6	30.7	5.2	5.0	11.7 [c]
	Money (M1)	28.2	28.9	22.2	16.5	34.4	30.5	6.6	28.7	7.8	8.3 [c]
	M2	19.8	23.5	20.8	12.9	34.2	38.4	13.3	26.4	14.0	14.0
	Foreign-currency deposits	12.7	-0.7	0.1	0.9	9.3	21.1	40.1	16.4	13.5	15.0
Peru	Monetary base	7.2	19.6	27.8	17.1	25.2	38.2	2.1	24.2	31.3	30.3
	Money (M1)	10.9	22.9	29.0	17.1	30.6	31.3	8.8	28.0	19.9	18.6
	M2	10.3	17.1	28.9	7.7	37.7	48.5	-2.2	27.8	18.8	22.7
	Foreign-currency deposits	-1.5	-3.3	2.5	11.4	7.9	11.2	23.1	-0.1	14.1	0.9
Saint Kitts and Nevis	Monetary base	-9.1	5.5	16.1	8.1	15.7	7.3	48.3	-3.2	36.1	...
	Money (M1)	12.7	16.1	8.8	6.5	17.4	7.2	9.2	19.5	25.7	20.6 [c]
	M2	6.0	15.6	12.4	6.7	12.5	9.9	10.4	10.2	9.5	9.6
	Foreign-currency deposits	11.9	11.6	18.8	17.5	16.4	-9.2	-7.0	-9.2	-0.7	-0.7
Saint Lucia	Monetary base	12.3	8.1	-10.0	7.8	14.4	10.2	8.5	3.6	16.3	...
	Money (M1)	21.6	26.5	11.1	9.6	5.0	7.1	-2.4	-4.3	4.0	2.6 [b]
	M2	7.8	4.8	10.9	11.5	11.3	10.7	4.1	0.2	4.9	3.8
	Foreign-currency deposits	35.3	42.0	54.6	32.5	47.8	8.9	9.3	-13.2	16.4	13.6
Saint Vincent and the Grenadines	Monetary base	4.3	12.5	-7.7	14.3	4.5	2.0	-3.2	11.9	0.8	...
	Money (M1)	6.1	6.3	8.1	12.8	6.8	-1.4	-8.3	-0.5	-3.9	-2.3 [c]
	M2	...	...	4.1	6.7	9.5	1.9	0.8	2.2	1.9	-0.1
	Foreign-currency deposits	...	...	32.7	7.4	102.1	1.5	-6.5	-7.7	30.8	-0.8
Suriname	Monetary base	...	...	...	...	39.7	30.2	22.1	13.0	3.2	24.4 [c]
	Money (M1)	...	...	...	...	26.7	21.3	26.3	16.7	5.3	14.5 [c]
	M2	...	...	...	...	30.2	21.0	25.1	18.2	7.0	17.6
	Foreign-currency deposits	...	...	...	...	25.7	24.3	12.0	7.9	39.1	14.4
Trinidad and Tobago	Monetary base	9.9	-7.8	14.4	41.5	19.0	32.3	37.6	24.7	14.1	20.7 [b]
	Money (M1)	12.2	8.8	24.2	21.8	7.4	17.6	24.0	25.5	17.2	16.5 [b]
	M2	6.5	6.2	23.7	24.8	13.2	17.2	17.6	17.9	8.4	12.1
	Foreign-currency deposits	-5.1	33.1	10.9	11.8	36.4	21.1	32.2	7.9	-4.0	2.2
Uruguay	Monetary base	6.1	3.8	24.6	23.5	28.9	28.6	6.1	12.9	23.1	23.5
	Money (M1)	24.6	21.7	23.1	28.5	23.0	22.4	13.1	24.6	19.6	21.1 [c]
	M2	18.0	18.1	19.6	29.5	22.8	26.6	11.1	26.2	26.3	19.4
	Foreign-currency deposits	7.9	13.5	-15.3	2.9	2.2	4.5	25.7	0.2	7.1	15.0
Venezuela (Bolivarian Republic of)	Monetary base	48.1	54.0	48.0	61.7	65.5	39.5	18.3	24.5	27.0	35.9 [c]
	Money (M1)	61.5	60.6	50.2	105.5	66.8	24.3	28.8	27.5	44.8	61.9
	M2	43.7	54.0	52.6	61.9	60.2	16.9	28.3	18.0	37.6	57.0

Source: Economic Commission for Latin America and the Caribbean (ECLAC), on the basis of official figures.
[a] Figures as of October.
[b] Figures as of August.
[c] Figures as of September.
[d] Figures as of July.

Table A-23
LATIN AMERICA AND THE CARIBBEAN: DOMESTIC CREDIT
(Percentage variation with respect to the year-earlier period)

	2003	2004	2005	2006	2007	2008	2009	2010	2011	2012 [a]
Antigua and Barbuda	7.6	-0.5	2.6	9.3	17.3	12.5	19.9	0.5	-4.0	-2.9 [b]
Argentina	5.2	3.8	-3.1	-6.2	1.7	23.9	2.3	51.3	59.5	31.2 [c]
Bahamas	0.7	5.1	12.9	14.3	4.8	7.5	5.3	3.4	0.8	4.6 [c]
Barbados	...	12.0	20.4	10.4	8.4	9.9	6.6	0.9	-2.3	4.5 [d]
Belize	6.9	16.1	4.9	15.9	13.6	9.3	5.6	-0.3	-1.6	0.0 [c]
Bolivia (Plurinational State of)	5.5	1.9	2.4	-3.2	6.5	7.5	10.9	13.0	18.8	22.7 [e]
Brazil	18.3	13.6	14.0	19.4	19.9	19.5	14.1	18.6	18.4	16.0
Chile	6.3	10.6	12.4	10.5	15.6	18.4	6.6	-0.1	12.1	18.2 [c]
Colombia	13.8	11.5	11.2	16.1	15.4	15.7	14.3	20.9	15.0	16.3 [e]
Costa Rica	19.7	20.1	14.4	16.6	22.1	21.1	19.1	4.6	12.4	13.9 [c]
Dominica	-10.1	-1.2	0.3	3.7	-9.3	4.9	8.5	12.5	13.7	8.4 [b]
Dominican Republic	64.7	28.2	5.9	21.4	12.2	17.7	13.6	12.7	12.4	10.6
Ecuador	-11.5	8.2	13.6	9.3	18.2	1.7	20.8	33.6	31.5	22.8 [d]
El Salvador	6.0	8.7	43.1	8.6	12.4	11.3	2.4	2.2	3.5	10.2
Grenada	5.9	-0.3	-3.1	12.5	15.4	13.1	8.9	4.0	2.6	4.9 [b]
Guatemala	8.9	26.7	11.5	15.5	13.8	10.4	5.2	5.6	15.1	11.3
Guyana	-4.1	20.5	24.1	-6.7	28.9	15.8	4.5	-0.8	34.5	49.6 [c]
Haiti	31.0	11.4	8.1	5.3	0.1	7.8	9.7	-22.9	-17.0	0.4 [b]
Honduras	19.9	11.7	-6.9	34.4	49.0	27.1	6.7	10.0	10.9	19.2 [c]
Jamaica	24.5	12.1	7.7	-1.5	12.4	16.3	15.0	-3.4	-4.1	10.8 [b]
Mexico	16.9	6.9	10.6	13.5	21.6	8.7	16.7	10.6	11.3	10.8 [c]
Nicaragua	7.3	4.1	7.9	3.8	11.1	10.1	-2.1	-3.9	-7.3	22.0 [c]
Panama	-3.3	8.8	6.1	16.0	10.7	15.9	1.2	9.5	18.8	18.7 [c]
Paraguay [f]	-17.2	-4.1	10.0	13.9	25.2	51.5	31.8	36.1	28.2	22.6
Peru	8.8	12.1	6.1	23.2	38.0	9.4	9.9	23.9	12.3	8.9
Saint Kitts and Nevis	-0.4	17.5	21.3	16.7	9.9	3.0	6.2	6.7	-0.3	-7.6 [b]
Saint Lucia	-6.2	4.6	15.0	23.5	29.6	21.1	4.6	-0.3	2.9	6.0 [b]
Saint Vincent and the Grenadines	-3.7	10.0	2.4	11.9	16.5	9.5	7.0	1.5	-7.2	-4.2 [b]
Suriname	...	...	...	...	20.7	18.5	16.9	21.4	20.8	9.5 [c]
Trinidad and Tobago	1.3	-3.3	-5.3	-40.0	90.1	6.5	35.5	36.6	9.3	5.5 [b]
Uruguay	-10.7	-24.3	-27.2	3.9	8.9	3.2	-2.6	13.9	39.9	19.5 [c]
Venezuela (Bolivarian Republic of) [g]	37.3	62.8	59.3	82.7	51.6	22.0	28.4	13.7	36.0	56.3 [c]

Source: Economic Commission for Latin America and the Caribbean (ECLAC), on the basis of official figures.
[a] Figures as of October.
[b] Figures as of August.
[c] Figures as of September.
[d] Figures as of July.
[e] Figures as of June.
[f] Figures as of May.
[g] Credit granted to the private sector by the banking sector.

Table A-24
LATIN AMERICA AND THE CARIBBEAN: MONETARY POLICY RATES
(Average rates)

	2003	2004	2005	2006	2007	2008	2009	2010	2011	2012 [a]
Antigua and Barbuda	6.8	6.5	6.5	6.5	6.5	6.5	6.5	6.5	6.5	6.5 [b]
Argentina	9.3	1.5	6.0	7.3	9.1	11.3	14.0	12.3	11.8	12.7
Bahamas	5.8	5.8	5.3	5.3	5.3	5.3	5.3	5.3	4.8	4.5
Barbados	7.5	7.5	8.8	11.7	12.0	11.8	7.9	7.0	7.0	7.0 [b]
Belize	12.0	12.0	12.0	12.0	12.0	12.0	18.0	18.0	11.0	11.0 [c]
Bolivia (Plurinational State of)	...	...	...	5.0	6.2	9.2	7.0	3.0	4.0	4.0
Brazil	23.8	16.4	19.1	15.4	12.0	12.4	10.1	9.9	11.8	8.8
Chile	2.7	1.9	3.5	5.0	5.3	7.2	1.8	1.5	4.8	5.0
Colombia	7.0	6.8	6.3	6.6	8.8	9.8	5.8	3.2	4.0	5.1
Costa Rica	...	...	...	8.8	6.0	8.0	9.6	8.1	5.6	5.0
Dominica	6.8	6.5	6.5	6.5	6.5	6.5	6.5	6.5	6.5	6.5 [b]
Dominican Republic	...	25.0	7.6	9.2	7.3	9.0	5.1	4.2	6.4	6.1
Grenada	6.8	6.5	6.5	6.5	6.5	6.5	6.5	6.5	6.5	6.5 [b]
Guatemala	...	...	3.3	4.7	5.5	6.9	5.5	4.5	4.9	5.3
Guyana	5.5	5.8	6.0	6.4	6.5	6.6	6.9	6.4	5.4	5.4 [c]
Haiti	26.3	15.6	12.7	18.2	11.6	6.9	6.2	5.0	3.2	3.0
Honduras	...	...	6.9	6.4	6.3	8.4	4.9	4.5	4.8	6.6
Jamaica	14.6	14.2	12.8	12.3	11.7	14.1	14.8	9.0	6.6	6.3 [c]
Mexico	6.2	6.8	9.2	7.2	7.2	7.8	5.7	4.5	4.5	4.5
Paraguay	15.5	6.6	4.8	9.7	6.0	5.9	2.1	2.2	8.0	6.1
Peru	3.2	2.7	3.0	4.3	4.7	5.9	3.3	2.1	4.0	4.3
Saint Kitts and Nevis	6.8	6.5	6.5	6.5	6.5	6.5	6.5	6.5	6.5	6.5 [b]
Saint Lucia	6.8	6.5	6.5	6.5	6.5	6.5	6.5	6.5	6.5	6.5 [b]
Saint Vincent and the Grenadines	6.8	6.5	6.5	6.5	6.5	6.5	6.5	6.5	6.5	6.5 [b]
Trinidad and Tobago	5.2	5.0	5.5	7.3	8.0	8.4	7.5	4.7	3.2	3.0
Uruguay	...	...	...	...	...	7.4	8.5	6.3	7.5	8.8
Venezuela (Bolivarian Republic of)	19.7	12.9	11.8	9.8	9.8	12.3	8.1	6.3	6.4	6.4 [c]

Source: Economic Commission for Latin America and the Caribbean (ECLAC), on the basis of official figures.
[a] Figures as of October.
[b] Figures as of July.
[c] Figures as of September.

Table A-25
LATIN AMERICA AND THE CARIBBEAN: REPRESENTATIVE LENDING RATES
(Average rates)

	2003	2004	2005	2006	2007	2008	2009	2010	2011	2012 [a]
Antigua and Barbuda [b]	13.4	11.5	11.2	10.7	10.3	10.1	9.5	10.2	10.1	9.6 [c]
Argentina [d]	16.8	10.8	10.5	12.9	14.0	19.8	21.3	15.2	17.7	19.4
Bahamas [b]	12.0	11.2	10.3	10.0	10.6	11.0	10.6	11.0	11.0	10.8 [e]
Barbados [b]	10.2	9.9	10.3	10.7	10.7	10.4	9.8	9.5	9.3	8.7 [f]
Belize [b]	14.3	13.9	14.3	14.2	14.3	14.1	14.1	13.9	13.4	12.6 [e]
Bolivia (Plurinational State of) [g]	21.0	17.2	12.1	8.8	8.3	8.9	8.5	5.2	6.3	6.7
Brazil [h]	49.8	41.1	43.7	40.0	34.5	38.8	40.4	38.5	40.7	33.5
Chile [i]	13.0	11.0	13.5	14.4	13.6	15.2	12.9	11.8	12.4	13.5
Colombia [b]	15.2	15.1	14.6	12.9	15.4	17.2	13.0	9.4	11.2	12.7
Costa Rica [j]	26.2	23.4	24.0	22.7	17.3	16.7	21.6	19.4	17.6	18.9
Cuba [k]	9.6	9.7	9.8	9.4	9.1	9.0	9.3	9.3	...	...
Dominica [b]	11.8	8.9	9.9	9.5	9.2	9.1	10.0	9.4	8.7	8.8 [c]
Dominican Republic [l]	27.8	30.3	21.4	15.7	11.7	16.0	12.9	8.3	11.7	12.6
Ecuador [m]	12.6	10.2	8.7	8.9	10.1	9.8	9.2	9.0	8.3	8.2
El Salvador [n]	6.6	6.3	6.9	7.5	7.8	7.9	9.3	7.6	6.0	5.6
Grenada [b]	10.3	10.3	10.0	9.8	9.7	9.4	10.7	10.3	10.4	9.8 [c]
Guatemala [b]	15.0	13.8	13.0	12.8	12.8	13.4	13.8	13.3	13.4	13.5
Guyana [l]	16.6	16.6	15.1	14.9	14.1	13.9	14.0	15.2	14.7	14.5 [e]
Haiti [o]	30.7	34.1	27.1	29.5	31.2	23.3	21.6	20.7	19.8	19.5
Honduras [b]	20.8	19.9	18.8	17.4	16.6	17.9	19.4	18.9	18.6	18.3
Jamaica [j]	25.1	25.1	23.2	22.0	22.0	22.3	22.6	20.3	18.3	17.9
Mexico [p]	7.0	7.4	9.7	7.5	7.6	8.7	7.1	5.3	4.9	4.7
Nicaragua [q]	15.5	13.5	12.1	11.6	13.0	13.2	14.0	13.3	10.8	12.1
Panama [r]	8.9	8.2	8.2	8.1	8.3	8.2	8.3	7.9	7.3	7.0
Paraguay [b]	30.5	21.2	15.3	16.6	14.6	14.6	15.6	13.2	16.3	15.6
Peru [s]	21.0	24.7	25.5	23.9	22.9	23.7	21.0	19.0	18.7	19.2
Saint Kitts and Nevis [b]	12.0	10.0	9.9	9.2	9.3	8.6	8.6	8.5	9.0	8.6 [c]
Saint Lucia [b]	15.3	10.8	10.4	10.5	9.9	9.3	9.0	9.5	9.2	8.5 [c]
Saint Vincent and the Grenadines [b]	12.0	9.7	9.6	9.7	9.6	9.5	9.1	9.0	9.0	9.2 [c]
Suriname [t]	21.0	20.4	18.1	15.6	13.8	12.0	11.7	11.7	11.8	11.7 [e]
Trinidad and Tobago [l]	11.0	9.4	9.1	10.2	10.5	12.3	11.9	9.2	8.0	7.8
Uruguay [u]	56.6	26.0	15.3	10.7	10.0	13.1	16.6	12.0	11.0	12.0
Venezuela (Bolivarian Republic of) [v]	25.7	17.3	15.6	14.6	16.7	22.8	20.6	18.0	17.4	16.3

Source: Economic Commission for Latin America and the Caribbean (ECLAC), on the basis of official figures.
[a] Figures as of October.
[b] Weighted average of the system lending rates.
[c] Figures as of June.
[d] Local-currency loans at fixed or renegotiable rates, signature loans of up to 89 days.
[e] Figures as of September.
[f] Figures as of July.
[g] Nominal local-currency rate for 60-91-day operations.
[h] Preset lending rates for legal persons.
[i] Lending rates for 90-360 days, non-adjustable operations.
[j] Average lending rate.
[k] Corporate lending rate in convertible pesos.
[l] Prime lending rate.
[m] Effective benchmark lending rate for the corporate commercial segment.
[n] Basic lending rate for up to 1 year.
[o] Average of minimum and maximum lending rates.
[p] Weighted average rate of private debt issues of up to 1 year, expressed as a 28-day curve.
Includes only stock certificates.
[q] Short-term loans rate, weighted average.
[r] Interest rate on 1-year trade credit.
[s] Market lending rate, average for transactions conducted in the last 30 business days.
[t] Average bank lending rate in local currency.
[u] Business credit, 30-367 days.
[v] Average rate for loan operations for the six major commercial banks.

Economic Commission for Latin America and the Caribbean (ECLAC)

Table A-26
LATIN AMERICA AND THE CARIBBEAN: CONSUMER PRICES
(12-month percentage variation)

	2003	2004	2005	2006	2007	2008	2009	2010	2011	2012 [a]
Latin America and the Caribbean [b]	**8.2**	**7.3**	**6.1**	**5.1**	**6.5**	**8.1**	**4.6**	**6.5**	**6.9**	**5.8**
Antigua and Barbuda	1.8	2.8	2.5	0.0	5.2	0.7	2.4	2.9	4.0	1.9 [c]
Argentina	3.7	6.1	12.3	9.8	8.5	7.2	7.7	10.9	9.5	10.2
Bahamas	2.4	1.9	1.2	2.3	2.8	4.6	1.3	1.4	3.2	2.3 [d]
Barbados	0.3	4.3	7.4	5.6	4.7	7.3	4.4	6.5	9.6	4.4 [e]
Belize	2.3	3.1	4.2	2.9	4.1	4.4	-0.4	0.0	2.6	0.5 [c]
Bolivia (Plurinational State of)	3.9	4.6	4.9	4.9	11.7	11.8	0.3	7.2	6.9	4.3
Brazil	9.3	7.6	5.7	3.1	4.5	5.9	4.3	5.9	6.5	5.5
Chile	1.1	2.4	3.7	2.6	7.8	7.1	-1.4	3.0	4.4	2.9
Colombia	6.5	5.5	4.9	4.5	5.7	7.7	2.0	3.2	3.7	3.1
Costa Rica	9.9	13.1	14.1	9.4	10.8	13.9	4.0	5.8	4.7	4.7
Cuba [f]	-3.8	2.9	3.7	5.7	10.6	-0.1	-0.1	1.5	2.7	2.1 [d]
Dominica	2.8	0.8	2.7	1.8	6.0	2.0	3.2	2.3	1.3	1.7 [d]
Dominican Republic	42.7	28.7	7.4	5.0	8.9	4.5	5.7	6.3	7.8	2.8
Ecuador	6.1	1.9	3.1	2.9	3.3	8.8	4.3	3.3	5.4	4.9
El Salvador	2.5	5.4	4.3	4.9	4.9	5.5	-0.2	2.1	5.1	1.0
Grenada	1.6	2.5	6.2	1.7	7.4	5.2	-2.3	4.2	3.5	1.3 [d]
Guatemala	5.9	9.2	8.6	5.8	8.7	9.4	-0.3	5.4	6.2	3.3
Guyana	5.0	5.5	8.2	4.2	14.1	6.4	3.6	4.5	3.3	1.9 [e]
Haiti	35.8	19.1	15.3	10.3	10.0	10.1	2.0	6.2	8.3	6.8
Honduras	6.8	9.2	7.7	5.3	8.9	10.8	3.0	6.5	5.6	5.7
Jamaica	13.8	13.6	12.6	5.6	16.8	16.9	10.2	11.8	6.0	7.2
Mexico	4.0	5.2	3.3	4.1	3.8	6.5	3.6	4.4	3.8	4.6
Nicaragua	6.6	8.9	9.7	10.2	16.2	12.7	1.8	9.1	8.6	6.8
Panama	1.4	-0.2	3.4	2.2	6.4	6.8	1.9	4.9	6.3	5.3
Paraguay	9.3	2.8	9.9	12.5	6.0	7.5	1.9	7.2	4.9	3.4
Peru	2.5	3.5	1.5	1.1	3.9	6.7	0.2	2.1	4.7	3.2
Saint Kitts and Nevis	3.0	1.6	6.2	8.0	2.9	6.5	1.2	5.2	2.9	2.1 [c]
Saint Lucia	2.2	1.7	3.9	4.8	8.3	8.7	-1.6	0.9	4.7	1.9 [d]
Saint Vincent and the Grenadines	0.5	3.5	5.2	-0.5	6.8	3.4	-3.1	4.2	4.8	3.0 [d]
Suriname	...	...	15.8	4.7	8.3	9.4	1.3	10.3	15.3	3.7 [c]
Trinidad and Tobago	3.0	5.6	7.2	9.1	7.6	14.5	1.3	13.4	5.3	7.7 [c]
Uruguay	10.2	7.6	4.9	6.4	8.5	9.2	5.9	6.9	8.6	9.1
Venezuela (Bolivarian Republic of)	27.1	19.2	14.4	17.0	22.5	31.9	26.9	27.4	29.0	18.5

Source: Economic Commission for Latin America and the Caribbean (ECLAC), on the basis of official figures.
[a] Twelve-month variation to October 2012.
[b] The only English-speaking Caribbean countries included are Barbados, Jamaica and Trinidad and Tobago.
[c] Twelve-month variation to September 2012.
[d] Twelve-month variation to August 2012.
[e] Twelve-month variation to June 2012.
[f] Refers to national-currency markets.

Table A-27
LATIN AMERICA AND THE CARIBBEAN: CENTRAL GOVERNMENT BALANCE
(Percentages of GDP, end-of-period stocks)

	Primary balance				Overall balance			
	2009	2010	2011	2012 [a]	2009	2010	2011	2012 [a]
Latin America and the Caribbean [b]	**-0.7**	**0.2**	**0.1**	**-0.4**	**-3.4**	**-2.3**	**-2.2**	**-2.9**
Latin America [c]	**-0.9**	**-0.1**	**0.2**	**-0.3**	**-2.7**	**-1.7**	**-1.6**	**-2.0**
The Caribbean [d]	**-0.2**	**0.7**	**-0.1**	**-0.5**	**-4.2**	**-2.9**	**-3.6**	**-4.0**
Antigua and Barbuda	-8.0	1.4	-2.7	-2.3	-10.9	-1.2	-5.3	-4.5
Argentina [e]	1.4	1.5	-0.1	0.5	-0.8	-0.1	-2.3	-1.6
Bahamas	-0.9	-1.1	0.1	-1.2	-3.2	-3.8	-2.6	-3.8
Barbados [f]	-3.5	-2.3	0.9	0.5	-8.3	-7.8	-5.2	-5.8
Belize	0.8	1.8	3.3	1.9	-2.8	-1.6	-0.3	-2.0
Bolivia (Plurinational State of) [f]	1.7	3.3	2.0	2.7	0.1	1.7	0.8	1.5
Brazil	1.2	2.1	2.3	1.8	-3.5	-1.7	-2.6	-2.2
Chile	-3.7	0.1	1.9	0.4	-4.2	-0.4	1.3	-0.2
Colombia	-1.1	-1.1	-0.1	0.3	-4.1	-3.9	-2.8	-2.4
Costa Rica	-1.3	-3.0	-1.9	-2.2	-3.4	-5.2	-4.1	-4.5
Cuba	-3.8	-2.2	...	...	-4.9	-3.6	...	...
Dominica	-1.0	3.0	-8.0	-8.2	-2.1	1.3	-9.8	-9.9
Dominican Republic	-1.6	-0.6	-0.5	-4.3	-3.5	-2.5	-2.6	-6.8
Ecuador	-3.5	-1.2	-0.8	-2.3	-4.3	-2.2	-1.8	-3.4
El Salvador	-1.2	-0.4	-0.1	2.0	-3.7	-2.7	-2.3	0.1
Grenada	-2.7	0.2	-0.7	-1.2	-4.9	-1.7	-3.0	-3.5
Guatemala	-1.7	-1.8	-1.3	-0.6	-3.1	-3.3	-2.8	-2.2
Guyana	-2.1	-1.2	-1.6	-3.4	-3.7	-2.9	-3.1	-4.6
Haiti	-0.7	1.8	0.2	...	-1.3	1.3	-0.1	...
Honduras	-5.5	-3.8	-1.7	-1.7	-6.2	-4.8	-2.9	-2.9
Jamaica	6.3	4.7	3.9	3.1	-11.4	-6.4	-5.9	-6.2
Mexico [g]	-0.4	-1.0	-0.7	-0.6	-2.3	-2.8	-2.5	-2.4
Nicaragua	-0.7	0.4	1.6	1.3	-1.7	-0.8	0.5	0.2
Panama [f]	1.9	0.8	0.1	-0.4	-1.0	-1.9	-2.2	-2.8
Paraguay	0.1	1.6	1.0	-2.5	0.1	1.2	0.7	-2.8
Peru	-0.2	1.1	1.9	1.7	-1.5	0.0	0.9	0.8
Saint Kitts and Nevis	6.0	2.9	6.8	8.8	-0.6	-4.1	0.8	2.2
Saint Lucia	0.8	2.2	-3.2	-3.0	-2.1	-0.6	-6.0	-6.4
Saint Vincent and the Grenadines	0.0	-0.8	-1.2	0.5	-2.7	-3.7	-3.6	-2.0
Suriname	5.2	-3.7	1.5	0.4	3.7	-5.2	-0.2	-0.8
Trinidad and Tobago	-3.2	2.2	-0.8	-2.2	-6.0	-0.2	-2.8	-4.4
Uruguay	1.3	1.3	1.9	0.1	-1.5	-1.2	-0.6	-2.3
Venezuela (Bolivarian Republic of)	-3.7	-2.1	-1.8	-1.3	-5.0	-3.6	-4.0	-3.8

Source: Economic Commission for Latin America and the Caribbean (ECLAC), on the basis of official figures.
[a] Preliminary figures prepared on the basis of information from budgets for 2013.
[b] Simple averages of the figures for 33 countries.
[c] Simple averages. Includes information on 19 countries of Latin America and the Caribbean: Argentina, Bolivarian Republic of Venezuela, Brazil, Chile, Colombia, Costa Rica, Dominican Republic, Ecuador, El Salvador, Guatemala, Haiti, Honduras, Mexico, Nicaragua, Panama, Paraguay, Peru, Plurinational State of Bolivia and Uruguay.
[d] Simple averages. Includes information on 13 Caribbean countries: Antigua and Barbuda, Bahamas, Barbados, Belize, Dominica, Grenada, Guyana, Jamaica, Saint Kitts and Nevis, Saint Lucia, Saint Vincent and the Grenadines, Suriname and Trinidad and Tobago.
[e] National public administration.
[f] Non-financial public sector.
[g] Public sector.

Economic Commission for Latin America and the Caribbean (ECLAC)

Table A-28
LATIN AMERICA AND THE CARIBBEAN: CENTRAL GOVERNMENT REVENUES
(Percentages of GDP, end-of-period stocks)

	Total revenue				Tax revenue			
	2009	2010	2011	2012 [a]	2009	2010	2011	2012 [a]
Latin America and the Caribbean [b]	**23.6**	**23.8**	**24.2**	**24.3**	**17.6**	**17.8**	**18.3**	**18.6**
Latin America [c]	**19.3**	**20.0**	**20.4**	**20.9**	**14.0**	**14.4**	**14.9**	**15.5**
The Caribbean [d]	**27.9**	**27.8**	**28.3**	**28.2**	**22.5**	**22.6**	**23.1**	**23.0**
Antigua and Barbuda	18.3	22.4	20.6	19.7	17.5	18.5	18.3	18.2
Argentina [e]	21.0	22.5	21.8	23.4	18.2	19.6	19.9	21.4
Bahamas	16.9	18.4	20.2	20.6	14.4	16.7	18.0	17.9
Barbados [f]	27.6	27.5	29.1	28.5	25.1	25.7	27.4	26.8
Belize	26.0	27.6	28.0	27.3	21.5	23.1	23.4	22.4
Bolivia (Plurinational State of) [f]	45.0	44.2	45.5	51.0	17.2	17.3	18.5	20.7
Brazil	22.8	24.3	23.8	24.5	22.8	24.3	23.8	24.5
Chile	19.0	21.7	22.9	22.1	15.2	17.3	18.9	19.0
Colombia	15.3	13.8	15.3	16.2	12.9	12.3	13.6	14.5
Costa Rica	14.0	14.4	14.6	14.7	13.8	13.4	13.7	13.5
Cuba	49.1	45.4	...	...	21.4	17.8	...	...
Dominica	31.7	32.3	29.9	...	24.7	25.7	23.9	...
Dominican Republic	13.7	13.6	13.5	13.9	13.1	12.8	12.9	13.3
Ecuador	18.8	25.8	25.5	27.1	11.7	14.9	14.5	16.4
El Salvador	13.8	15.0	15.4	16.7	12.6	13.4	13.9	15.2
Granada	20.6	23.6	22.1	19.4	18.1	18.6	18.3	17.1
Guatemala	11.1	11.2	11.8	11.6	10.6	10.8	11.4	10.8
Guyana	27.2	26.0	25.6	28.4	21.6	21.9	21.2	20.3
Haiti	12.1	15.7	14.3	...	11.7	11.9	13.1	...
Honduras	17.5	17.4	17.5	17.1	14.6	14.8	15.3	15.4
Jamaica	28.1	27.3	26.1	24.8	24.9	24.3	23.4	22.2
Mexico [g]	23.7	22.7	22.9	23.6	9.5	9.7	9.1	9.8
Nicaragua	16.4	16.9	18.0	18.4	13.5	14.2	15.2	15.5
Panama [f]	25.9	25.4	24.8	25.9	10.9	11.4	11.3	11.8
Paraguay	17.6	17.1	17.7	19.4	11.6	12.0	12.3	13.1
Peru	15.6	17.0	17.8	18.5	13.4	14.5	15.2	15.7
Saint Kitts and Nevis	33.5	31.7	39.3	39.8	21.2	18.9	21.7	24.0
Saint Lucia	25.1	26.0	23.9	25.5	22.8	22.3	21.4	22.9
Saint Vincent and the Grenadines	28.5	26.5	26.5	27.0	23.4	22.4	22.2	23.3
Suriname	49.1	39.0	43.0	44.9	31.1	28.1	32.4	33.4
Trinidad and Tobago	30.6	32.5	33.0	31.1	26.6	27.9	29.2	26.8
Uruguay	21.0	21.2	21.1	20.8	18.6	18.5	18.8	18.8
Venezuela (Bolivarian Republic of)	21.4	19.3	22.5	18.8	13.3	11.1	12.5	11.9

Source: Economic Commission for Latin America and the Caribbean (ECLAC), on the basis of official figures.
[a] Preliminary figures prepared on the basis of information from budgets for 2013.
[b] Simple averages of the figures for 33 countries.
[c] Simple averages. Includes information on 19 countries of Latin America and the Caribbean: Argentina, Bolivarian Republic of Venezuela, Brazil, Chile, Colombia, Costa Rica, Dominican Republic, Ecuador, El Salvador, Guatemala, Haiti, Honduras, Mexico, Nicaragua, Panama, Paraguay, Peru, Plurinational State of Bolivia and Uruguay.
[d] Simple averages. Includes information on 13 Caribbean countries: Antigua and Barbuda, Bahamas, Barbados, Belize, Dominica, Grenada, Guyana, Jamaica, Saint Kitts and Nevis, Saint Lucia, Saint Vincent and the Grenadines, Suriname and Trinidad and Tobago.
[e] National public administration.
[f] Non-financial public sector.
[g] Public sector.

Table A-29
LATIN AMERICA AND THE CARIBBEAN: CENTRAL GOVERNMENT EXPENDITURE
(Percentages of GDP, end-of-period stocks)

	Total expenditure				Public-debt interest payments				Capital expenditure			
	2009	2010	2011	2012 [a]	2009	2010	2011	2012 [a]	2009	2010	2011	2012 [a]
Latin America and the Caribbean [b]	**26.9**	**26.1**	**26.4**	**27.2**	**2.6**	**2.4**	**2.5**	**2.5**	**5.3**	**4.8**	**5.0**	**5.1**
Latin America [c]	**21.9**	**21.7**	**21.9**	**22.9**	**1.8**	**1.7**	**1.8**	**1.8**	**4.5**	**4.6**	**4.6**	**5.1**
The Caribbean [d]	**32.2**	**30.7**	**31.9**	**32.2**	**4.0**	**3.6**	**3.5**	**3.6**	**6.3**	**5.0**	**5.7**	**5.2**
Antigua and Barbuda	29.2	23.6	25.9	24.1	2.9	2.5	2.6	2.1	5.3	1.7	2.2	1.7
Argentina [e]	21.8	22.6	24.1	25.0	2.3	1.6	2.2	2.1	2.7	3.1	3.0	2.8
Bahamas	20.1	22.3	22.8	24.4	2.3	2.7	2.7	2.7	2.0	2.7	2.9	3.5
Barbados [f]	36.0	35.4	34.3	34.3	4.8	5.5	6.1	6.3	3.2	2.1	1.1	1.3
Belize	28.8	29.2	28.3	29.2	3.6	3.4	3.6	3.8	4.2	4.8	3.5	4.7
Bolivia (Plurinational State of) [f]	44.9	43.1	44.7	49.5	1.6	1.6	1.2	1.2	12.8	10.7	13.3	16.0
Brazil	26.2	26.0	26.4	26.6	4.7	3.8	4.9	4.0	4.5	5.9	4.8	...
Chile	23.2	22.1	21.6	22.3	0.5	0.5	0.6	0.6	4.4	4.0	4.1	4.1
Colombia	19.4	17.7	18.1	18.6	3.0	2.7	2.7	2.8	2.3	1.9	2.9	2.9
Costa Rica	17.4	19.6	18.7	19.1	2.1	2.1	2.2	2.3	1.8	2.4	1.5	...
Cuba	53.9	49.0	...	...	1.1	1.3	...	...	8.2	6.1	...	...
Dominica	33.8	31.0	39.7	...	1.1	1.6	1.8	...	11.6	6.9	14.7	...
Dominican Republic	16.9	16.4	16.1	20.7	1.9	1.9	2.1	2.5	3.6	3.8	3.6	6.0
Ecuador	23.0	28.0	27.3	30.5	0.8	1.0	1.0	1.1	8.6	11.3	11.9	13.3
El Salvador	17.6	17.7	17.7	16.6	2.5	2.3	2.2	1.9	2.9	3.2	3.1	3.2
Grenada	25.5	25.2	25.1	22.9	2.2	1.9	2.3	2.2	5.6	5.6	6.0	5.1
Guatemala	14.2	14.5	14.7	13.7	1.4	1.5	1.5	1.5	4.1	4.1	4.0	3.1
Guyana	30.8	28.9	28.7	33.0	1.6	1.7	1.5	1.2	11.4	10.1	9.5	13.2
Haiti	13.3	14.4	14.3	...	0.5	0.5	0.3	...	2.2	3.7	2.3	...
Honduras	23.8	22.2	20.4	20.0	0.7	1.0	1.3	1.2	5.3	3.8	3.1	3.3
Jamaica	39.5	33.7	32.0	31.0	17.7	11.1	9.7	9.3	4.1	3.5	3.9	...
Mexico [g]	26.0	25.6	25.4	26.1	1.9	1.9	1.8	1.8	5.1	5.1	4.9	5.5
Nicaragua	18.2	17.6	17.6	18.2	1.0	1.1	1.1	1.1	4.1	4.0	3.7	3.8
Panama [f]	27.0	27.3	27.0	28.6	3.0	2.6	2.4	2.4	7.2	8.3	8.6	...
Paraguay	17.5	15.9	17.0	22.2	0.0	0.4	0.3	0.3	4.1	3.4	4.0	4.9
Peru	17.1	16.9	16.9	17.8	1.2	1.1	1.0	1.0	3.7	4.3	4.1	4.1
Saint Kitts and Nevis	34.0	35.7	38.5	37.7	6.5	6.9	6.0	6.6	5.1	6.8	4.5	3.9
Saint Lucia	27.2	26.6	30.0	32.0	2.8	2.8	2.8	3.4	6.3	4.5	8.2	7.6
Saint Vincent and the Grenadines	31.2	30.2	30.2	28.9	2.6	2.8	2.4	2.5	5.8	4.0	3.4	3.0
Suriname	45.4	44.3	43.2	45.7	1.5	1.5	1.7	1.2	10.1	8.3	8.5	7.3
Trinidad and Tobago	36.7	32.7	35.8	35.4	2.8	2.4	2.0	2.1	6.4	4.5	5.3	5.4
Uruguay	22.6	22.4	21.7	23.1	2.8	2.4	2.5	2.4	1.6	1.7	1.5	1.6
Venezuela (Bolivarian Republic of)	26.5	22.9	26.4	22.6	1.3	1.5	2.1	2.5	5.4	2.9	3.1	4.6

Source: Economic Commission for Latin America and the Caribbean (ECLAC), on the basis of official figures.
[a] Preliminary figures prepared on the basis of information from budgets for 2013.
[b] Simple averages of the figures for 33 countries.
[c] Simple averages. Includes information on 19 countries of Latin America and the Caribbean: Argentina, Bolivarian Republic of Venezuela, Brazil, Chile, Colombia, Costa Rica, Dominican Republic, Ecuador, El Salvador, Guatemala, Haiti, Honduras, Mexico, Nicaragua, Panama, Paraguay, Peru, Plurinational State of Bolivia and Uruguay.
[d] Simple averages. Includes information on 13 Caribbean countries: Antigua and Barbuda, Bahamas, Barbados, Belize, Dominica, Grenada, Guyana, Jamaica, Saint Kitts and Nevis, Saint Lucia, Saint Vincent and the Grenadines, Suriname and Trinidad and Tobago.
[e] National public administration.
[f] Non-financial public sector.
[g] Public sector.

Table A-30
LATIN AMERICA AND THE CARIBBEAN: GROSS PUBLIC-DEBT
(Percentages of GDP, end-of-period stocks)

	Central government				Non-financial public sector			
	2009	2010	2011	2012 [a]	2009	2010	2011	2012 [a]
Latin America and the Caribbean [b]	...	...	...	...	**51.0**	**51.4**	**50.8**	...
Latin America [c]	**31.0**	**30.4**	**30.5**	**29.9**	**33.7**	**32.6**	**32.5**	...
The Caribbean [d]	...	...	...	...	**76.2**	**78.9**	**77.7**	...
Antigua and Barbuda	...	...	...	...	95.7	87.1	86.7	...
Argentina	48.5	45.1	41.6	39.9	53.6	45.3	42.2	...
Bahamas	...	...	...	...	50.0	61.8	60.2	49.9
Barbados	...	...	...	...	84.1	98.5	95.9	106.4
Belize	...	...	...	...	82.2	72.3	70.7	75.5
Bolivia (Plurinational State of)	36.3	34.5	34.4	29.1	39.5	38.1	34.5	29.2
Brazil	60.9	53.4	54.2	57.8	60.9	53.4	54.2	57.8
Chile	6.1	11.1	12.8	11.3	12.7	19.1	20.4	18.9
Colombia	35.0	35.0	33.8	32.0	45.1	46.2	43.4	39.8
Costa Rica	27.4	29.2	30.9	31.3	34.0	35.8	38.5	38.5
Dominica	...	...	...	...	66.4	73.1	70.7	...
Dominican Republic	28.2	29.2	30.1	31.8	28.7	29.5	30.4	32.3
Ecuador	15.3	21.6	21.3	20.9	16.5	21.5	21.4	22.3
El Salvador	42.6	42.5	41.9	42.2	45.2	45.1	44.3	44.6
Grenada	...	...	...	...	90.0	91.8	86.8	...
Guatemala	22.9	24.1	24.1	24.5	23.3	24.4	24.3	24.7
Guyana	...	...	...	...	60.5	61.2	78.8	...
Haiti	34.4	23.1	24.6	26.8	35.1	23.2	24.6	26.9
Honduras	24.5	30.0	31.9	32.1	22.9	25.4	27.6	27.7
Jamaica	...	...	...	...	139.8	139.0	126.0	130.5
Mexico	28.1	27.6	28.4	28.8	34.9	34.1	35.5	35.2
Nicaragua	33.6	34.6	33.4	31.7	34.6	35.5	34.2	32.5
Panama	44.7	42.3	40.3	39.4	45.4	43.0	40.9	39.9
Paraguay	14.4	13.9	11.9	11.0	16.8	14.6	12.5	12.2
Peru	23.4	21.3	19.0	17.1	23.7	21.5	19.2	17.8
Saint Kitts and Nevis	...	...	...	...	142.0	151.4	141.1	...
Saint Lucia	...	...	...	...	64.0	65.5	66.3	...
Saint Vincent and the Grenadines	...	...	...	...	64.7	66.7	63.7	...
Suriname	...	...	...	...	18.5	21.6	24.2	27.7
Trinidad and Tobago	...	...	...	...	32.9	36.2	38.4	46.6
Uruguay	44.7	39.3	40.0	39.4	49.0	42.8	43.9	43.9
Venezuela (Bolivarian Republic of)	18.2	20.2	25.1	21.4	18.2	20.2	25.1	21.4

Source: Economic Commission for Latin America and the Caribbean (ECLAC), on the basis of official figures.
[a] Preliminary figures to September.
[b] Simple averages of the figures for 33 countries.
[c] Simple averages. Includes information on 19 countries of Latin America and the Caribbean: Argentina, Bolivarian Republic of Venezuela, Brazil, Chile, Colombia, Costa Rica, Dominican Republic, Ecuador, El Salvador, Guatemala, Haiti, Honduras, Mexico, Nicaragua, Panama, Paraguay, Peru, Plurinational State of Bolivia and Uruguay.
[d] Simple averages. Includes information on 13 Caribbean countries: Antigua and Barbuda, Bahamas, Barbados, Belize, Dominica, Grenada, Guyana, Jamaica, Saint Kitts and Nevis, Saint Lucia, Saint Vincent and the Grenadines, Suriname and Trinidad and Tobago.

Naciones Unidas
United Nations

Publicaciones de la CEPAL / *ECLAC publications*

Comisión Económica para América Latina y el Caribe / *Economic Commission for Latin America and the Caribbean*
Casilla 179-D, Santiago de Chile. E-mail: publications@cepal.org
Véalas en: www.cepal.org/publicaciones
Publications may be accessed at: www.eclac.org

Revista CEPAL / *CEPAL Review*

La Revista se inició en 1976 como parte del Programa de Publicaciones de la Comisión Económica para América Latina y el Caribe, con el propósito de contribuir al examen de los problemas del desarrollo socioeconómico de la región. Las opiniones expresadas en los artículos firmados, incluidas las colaboraciones de los funcionarios de la Secretaría, son las de los autores y, por lo tanto, no reflejan necesariamente los puntos de vista de la Organización.

La *Revista CEPAL* se publica en español e inglés tres veces por año.

Los precios de suscripción anual vigentes son de US$ 30 para la versión en español y US$ 35 para la versión en inglés. El precio por ejemplar suelto es de US$ 15 para ambas versiones. Los precios de suscripción por dos años son de US$ 50 para la versión en español y US$ 60 para la versión en inglés.

CEPAL Review first appeared in 1976 as part of the Publications Programme of the Economic Commission for Latin America and the Caribbean, its aim being to make a contribution to the study of the economic and social development problems of the region. The views expressed in signed articles, including those by Secretariat staff members, are those of the authors and therefore do not necessarily reflect the point of view of the Organization.

CEPAL Review is published in Spanish and English versions three times a year.

Annual subscription costs are US$ 30 for the Spanish version and US$ 35 for the English version. The price of single issues is US$ 15 for both versions. The cost of a two-year subscription is US$ 50 for the Spanish version and US$ 60 for the English version.

Informes periódicos institucionales / *Annual reports*

Todos disponibles para años anteriores / *Issues for previous years also available*

- *Informe Macroeconómico de América Latina y el Caribe, junio de 2012*, 86 p.
- **Macroeconomic Report on Latin America and the Caribbean - June 2012, 80 p.**
- *Balance Preliminar de las Economías de América Latina y el Caribe 2012.* Documento informativo, 102 p.
  Preliminary Overview of the Economies of Latin America and the Caribbean 2012. Briefing paper, 98 p.
- *Estudio Económico de América Latina y el Caribe 2012*, 104 p.
  Economic Survey of Latin America and the Caribbean 2012, 100 p.
- *Panorama de la Inserción Internacional de América Latina y el Caribe 2011-2012*, 138 p.
  Latin America and the Caribbean in the World Economy 2011-2012, 116 p.
- *Panorama Social de América Latina, 2012.* Documento informativo, 60 p.
  Social Panorama of Latin America, 2012. Briefing paper, 58 p.
- *La Inversión Extranjera Directa en América Latina y el Caribe 2011*, 200 p.
  Foreign Direct Investment in Latin America and the Caribbean 2011, 184 p.
- *Anuario Estadístico de América Latina y el Caribe, 2012 /* **Statistical Yearbook for Latin America and the Caribbean, 2012**, 224 p.

Libros de la CEPAL

114 *China y América Latina y el Caribe. Hacia una relación económica y comercial estratégica*, Osvaldo Rosales y Mikio Kuwayama, 2012, 258 p.

114 **China *and Latin America and the Caribbean Building a strategic economic and trade relationship*, Osvaldo Rosales y Mikio Kuwayama, 2012, 244 p.**

113 *Competitividad, sostenibilidad e inclusión social en la agricultura: Nuevas direcciones en el diseño de políticas en América Latina y el Caribe,* Octavio Sotomayor, Adrián Rodríguez y Mônica Rodrigues, 2012, 352 p.

112 *El desarrollo inclusivo en América Latina y el Caribe.* Ensayos sobre políticas de convergencia productiva para la igualdad, Ricardo Infante (editor), 2011, 384 p.

111 *Protección social inclusiva en América Latina. Una mirada integral, un enfoque de derechos,* Simone Cecchini y Rodrigo Martínez, 2011, 284 p.

110 *Envejecimiento en América Latina. Sistema de pensiones y protección social integral,* Antonio Prado y Ana Sojo (eds.), 2010, 304 p.

109 **Modeling Public Policies in Latin America and the Caribbean, Carlos de Miguel, José Durán Lima, Paolo Giordiano, Julio Guzmán, Andrés Schuschny and Masazaku Watanuki (eds.), 2011, 322 p.**

108 *Alianzas público-privadas. Para una nueva visión estratégica del desarrollo,* Robert Devlin y Graciela Moguillansky, 2010, 196 p.

107 *Políticas de apoyo a las pymes en América Latina. Entre avances innovadores y desafíos institucionales,* Carlos Ferraro y Giovanni Stumpo, 2010, 392 p.

106 *Temas controversiales en negociaciones comerciales Norte-Sur,* Osvaldo Rosales V. y Sebastián Sáez C. (compiladores), 2011, 322 p.

105 **Regulation, Worker Protection and Active Labour-Market Policies in Latin America, Jürgen Weller (ed.), 2009, 236 p.**

104 *La República Dominicana en 2030: hacia una sociedad cohesionada,* Víctor Godínez y Jorge Máttar (coords.), 2009, 582 p.

103 **L'Amérique latine et les Caraïbes au seuil du troisième millénaire, 2009, 138 p.**

102 *Migración interna y desarrollo en América Latina entre 1980 y 2005,* Jorge Rodríguez y Gustavo Busso, 2009, 272 p.

101 *Claves de la innovación social en América Latina y el Caribe,* Adolfo Rodríguez Herrera y Hernán Alvarado Ugarte, 2009, 236 p.

Copublicaciones recientes / *Recent co-publications*

Sentido de pertenencia en sociedades fragmentadas. América Latina desde una perspectiva global, Martín Hopenhayn y Ana Sojo (comps.), CEPAL/Siglo Veintiuno, Argentina, 2011.

Las clases medias en América Latina. Retrospectiva y nuevas tendencias, Rolando Franco, Martín Hopenhayn y Arturo León (eds.), CEPAL/Siglo XXI, México, 2010.

Innovation and Economic Development. The Impact of Information and Communication Technologies in Latin America, Mario Cimoli, André Hofman and Nanno Mulder, ECLAC/Edward Elgar Publishing, United Kingdom, 2010.

Sesenta años de la CEPAL. Textos seleccionados del decenio 1998-2008, Ricardo Bielschowsky (comp.), CEPAL/Siglo Veintiuno, Argentina, 2010.

El nuevo escenario laboral latinoamericano. Regulación, protección y políticas activas en los mercados de trabajo, Jürgen Weller (ed.), CEPAL/Siglo Veintiuno, Argentina, 2010.

Internacionalización y expansión de las empresas eléctricas españolas en América Latina, Patricio Rozas, CEPAL/Lom, Chile, 2009.

Gobernanza corporativa y desarrollo de mercados de capitales en América Latina, Georgina Núñez, Andrés Oneto y Germano M. de Paula (coords.), CEPAL/Mayol, Colombia, 2009.

Coediciones recientes / *Recent co-editions*

Perspectivas económicas de América Latina 2013. Políticas de Pymes para el Cambio Estructural, OCDE/CEPAL, Chile, 2012.

Latin American Economic Outlook 2013. SME Policies For Structural Change, OECD/ECLAC, Chile, 2012.

Perspectivas de la agricultura y del desarrollo rural en las Américas: una mirada hacia América Latina y el Caribe 2013, CEPAL/FAO/IICA, Chile, 2012.

Reforma fiscal en América Latina. ¿Qué fiscalidad para qué desarrollo?, Alicia Bárcena y Narcís Serra (editores), CEPAL/SEGIB/CIDOB, Chile, 2012.

La sostenibilidad del desarrollo a 20 años de la Cumbre para la Tierra. Avances, brechas y lineamientos estratégicos para América Latina y el Caribe, CEPAL/Naciones Unidas, 2012.

Sustainable development 20 years on from the Earth Summit. Progress, gaps and strategic guidelines for Latin America and the Caribbean, ECLAC/United Nations, 2012.

Perspectivas económicas de América Latina 2012.Transformación del Estado para el desarrollo, CEPAL/OCDE, 2011.

Latin America Outlook 2012. Transforming the State for Development, ECLAC/OECD, 2011.

Perspectives économiques de l'Amérique latine 2012. Transformation de l'État et Développement, CEPALC/OCDE, 2012.

Breeding Latin American Tigers. Operational principles for rehabilitating industrial policies, Robert Devlin and Graciela Moguillansky, ECLAC/World Bank, 2011.

Espacios iberoamericanos: Hacia una nueva arquitectura del Estado para el desarrollo, CEPAL/SEGIB, 2011.

Espaços ibero-americanos: A uma nova arquitetura do Estado para o desenvolvimento. CEPAL/SEGIB, 2011.

Perspectivas de la agricultura y del desarrollo rural en las Américas: una mirada hacia América Latina y el Caribe, CEPAL/FAO/IICA, 2011.

The Oulook for Agriculture and Rural Development in the Americas: A Perspective on Latin America and the Caribbean, ECLAC/FAO/IICA, 2011.

Pobreza infantil en América Latina y el Caribe, CEPAL/UNICEF, Chile, 2010.

Espacios iberoamericanos: vínculos entre universidades y empresas para el desarrollo tecnológico, CEPAL/SEGIB, 2010.

Espaços ibero-Americanos: vínculos entre universidades e empresas para o desenvolvimento tecnológico, CEPAL/SEGIB, 2010.

Cuadernos de la CEPAL

100 *Construyendo autonomía. Compromiso e indicadores de género*, Karina Batthyáni Dighiero, 2012, 338 p.

99 *Si no se cuenta, no cuenta*, Diane Alméras y Coral Calderón Magaña (coords.), 2012, 394 p.

98 **Macroeconomic cooperation for uncertain times: The REDIMA experience**, Rodrigo Cárcamo-Díaz, 2012,164 p.

97 *El financiamiento de la infraestructura: Propuestas para el desarrollo sostenible de una política sectorial*, Patricio Rozas Balbontín, José Luis Bonifaz y Gustavo Guerra-García, 2012, 414 p.

96 *Una mirada a la crisis desde los márgenes*, Sonia Montaño (coord.), 2011, 102 p.

95 *Programas de transferencias condicionadas. Balance de la experiencia reciente en América Latina y el Caribe*, Simone Cecchini y Aldo Madariaga, 2011, 226 p.

95 **Conditional cash transfer programmes. The recent experience in Latin America and the Caribbean**, Simone Cecchini and Aldo Madariaga, 2011, 220 p.

94 *El cuidado en acción. Entre el derecho y el trabajo*, Sonia Montaño Virreira y Coral Calderón Magaña (coords.), 2010, 236 p.

93 *Privilegiadas y discriminadas. Las trabajadoras del sector financiero*, Flavia Marco Navarro y María Nieves Rico Ibáñez (eds.), 2009, 300 p.

Cuadernos estadísticos de la CEPAL

40 *América Latina y el Caribe: Índices de precios al consumidor. Serie enero de 1995 a junio de 2012. Solo disponible en CD*, 2012.

39 *América Latina y el Caribe: indicadores macroeconómicos del turismo. Solo disponible en CD*, 2010.

38 *Indicadores ambientales de América Latina y el Caribe, 2009. Solo disponible en CD*, 2010.

37 *América Latina y el Caribe: Series históricas de estadísticas económicas 1950-2008. Solo disponible en CD*, 2009.

36 *Clasificaciones estadísticas internacionales incorporadas en el Banco de Datos de Comercio Exterior de América Latina y el Caribe de la CEPAL (Revisión 3). Solo disponible en CD*, 2008.

Observatorio demográfico / *Demographic Observatory*

Edición bilingüe (español e inglés) que proporciona información estadística actualizada, referente a estimaciones y proyecciones de población de los países de América Latina y el Caribe. Incluye también indicadores demográficos de interés, tales como tasas de natalidad, mortalidad, esperanza de vida al nacer, distribución de la población, etc.

Desde 2013 el Observatorio aparece una vez al año. Valor por ejemplar: US$ 15.

Bilingual publication (Spanish and English) proving up-to-date estimates and projections of the populations of the Latin American and Caribbean countries. Also includes various demographic indicators of interest such as fertility and mortality rates, life expectancy, measures of population distribution, etc.

Since 2013, the Observatory appears once a year. Annual. Per issue: US$ 15.

Notas de población

Revista especializada que publica artículos e informes acerca de las investigaciones más recientes sobre la dinámica demográfica en la región, en español, con resúmenes en español e inglés. También incluye información sobre actividades científicas y profesionales en el campo de población.

La revista se publica desde 1973 y aparece dos veces al año, en junio y diciembre.

Suscripción anual: US$ 20. Valor por cada ejemplar: US$ 12.

Specialized journal which publishes articles and reports on recent studies of demographic dynamics in the region, in Spanish with abstracts in Spanish and English. Also includes information on scientific and professional activities in the field of population.

Published since 1973, the journal appears twice a year in June and December.

Annual subscription: US$ 20. Per issue: US$ 12.

Series de la CEPAL

*Comercio Internacional / Desarrollo Productivo / Desarrollo Territorial / Estudios Estadísticos y Prospectivos / Estudios y Perspectivas (Bogotá, Brasilia, Buenos Aires, México, Montevideo) / **Studies and Perspectives** (The Caribbean, Washington) / Financiamiento del Desarrollo / Gestión Pública / Informes y Estudios Especiales / Macroeconomía del Desarrollo / Manuales / Medio Ambiente y Desarrollo / Mujer y Desarrollo / Población y Desarrollo / Políticas Fiscales / Políticas Sociales / Recursos Naturales e Infraestructura / Reformas Económicas / Seminarios y Conferencias.*

Las publicaciones de la Comisión Económica para América Latina y el Caribe (CEPAL) y las del Instituto Latinoamericano y del Caribe de Planificación Económica y Social (ILPES) se pueden adquirir a los distribuidores locales o directamente a través de:

Publicaciones de las Naciones Unidas
2 United Nations Plaza, Room DC2-853
Nueva York, NY, 10017
Estados Unidos
Tel. (1 800)253-9646   Fax (1 212)963-3489
E-mail: publications@un.org

Publicaciones de las Naciones Unidas
Sección de Ventas
Palais des Nations
1211 Ginebra 10
Suiza
Tel. (41 22)917-2613   Fax (41 22)917-0027

Unidad de Distribución
Comisión Económica para América Latina y el Caribe (CEPAL)
Av. Dag Hammarskjöld 3477, Vitacura
7630412 Santiago
Chile
Tel. (56 2)210-2056   Fax (56 2)210-2069
E-mail: publications@cepal.org

Publications of the Economic Commission for Latin America and the Caribbean (ECLAC) and those of the Latin American and the Caribbean Institute for Economic and Social Planning (ILPES) can be ordered from your local distributor or directly through:

United Nations Publications
2 United Nations Plaza, Room DC2-853
New York, NY, 10017
USA
Tel. (1 800)253-9646   Fax (1 212)963-3489
E-mail: publications@un.org

United Nations Publications
Sales Sections
Palais des Nations
1211 Geneva 10
Switzerland
Tel. (41 22)917-2613   Fax (41 22)917-0027

Distribution Unit
Economic Commission for Latin America and the Caribbean (ECLAC)
Av. Dag Hammarskjöld 3477, Vitacura
7630412 Santiago
Chile
Tel. (56 2)210-2056   Fax (56 2)210-2069
E-mail: publications@eclac.org